Goodstone

Goodstone

Fred Voss

BLOODAXE BOOKS

Some of the poems in **Goodstone** have previously appeared in these magazines, anthologies and chapbooks:

A.K.A. Magazine
5 A.M.
Fred and Joan
Goodstone Aircraft Company
Guts
Invocation L.A.: Urban Multicultural Poetry
Men's Issues Anthology
Muses: Words Into Music
One Page
Pearl
Wordsworth's Socks
The Wormwood Review
Tsunami

Goodstone

Library of Congress Catalog Card Number 91-74039
ISBN 0-9627501-5-8

Printed in the United States of America.
First Printing, September 1991

Published by Event Horizon Press
Post Office Box 14645, Long Beach, California 90803

First published in Britain 1991 by
Bloodaxe Books Ltd,
P.O. Box 1SN,
Newcastle upon Tyne NE99 1SN.

ISBN: 1 85224 198 5

Bloodaxe Books Ltd acknowledges
the financial assistance of Northern Arts.

Many of the poems in **Goodstone** were
first published in Britain in *Bête Noire*.

Preface

For the last couple of years people have, with ever-increasing frequency, been announcing to me, "That Fred Voss guy is really a great poet!" Then they await my response. It's an awkward moment. Should I reply, "No kidding. Thanks for tipping me off. I'll read his stuff first chance I get." They either don't realize or have forgotten that I've been telling anyone who would listen what a talented and unique writer Fred is since first having the opportunity to read his manuscripts and to observe his dedicated literary work habits at least ten years ago. Fortunately the word has now gotten out, not only nationally but overseas. If you are not already one of Fred's fans, you are likely to be before you have read far into this collection. This machinist-by-trade welds innate verbal gifts, a solid education, the subtle ear of a true free-versifier, two decades of experience as a working man among working men, the aforementioned work ethic, and a balance of wit, irony, satire, compassion, and the absurd into icons of the American infrastructure.

So when you tell me, as tell me you will, what a damn fine poet Fred Voss is, don't be surprised when my jaw drops. The only person to whom I would never admit the dimensions of my respect for Fred and for his work is Fred. I value my friends so much that I devote myself to the preservation of their humility. I trust that when Fred sees my name on this Preface, he will assume it to be just more verbal abuse and will pass over it unread.

Gerry Locklin
Long Beach, 7-26-91

for my beautiful wife Joan

A Golden Opportunity

They stuck me on the rake
that stuck through a 2' x 2' cutout
in a 10' square oven
full of molten metal,
making me rake the orange searing lake
in tandem with a Mexican,
our skinny teenage arms around the 25' long rake handle
as we ran and pushed and pulled
backwards and forwards
making the lake of molten metal
lap against the walls
of the oven.
And the only time we weren't raking
was when we were
staggering
to the salt dispenser
on the wall in a corner
to gobble salt tablets to keep from passing out
from dehydration,
or when we were carrying shovels full
of metal boulders
to the oven and dumping them
through another 2' x 2' cutout
into the lake of molten metal.
As all the time
the forklift driver moved barrels
of the metal boulders around,
sitting high up against the thick leather seat
of his forklift and grinning
at my weakness
as it dawned on me that everyone working in the foundry
was either an illegal alien
or just out of County Jail
or State Prison,
and I realized
why the billboard
on top of the Employment Agency roof
had said FREE JOBS.

Emergency

The machinist steps on the gas,
risking his life and the lives of other drivers
as he swerves and darts in and out of traffic,
honking and turning red with his wristwatch in his
face, then jumping out of his car
and running across the street through traffic
to flash his badge as he races past the guard gate
and sprints for building 88,
throwing open the door and skidding to a halt
to jam his i.d. badge into the slot
of the time clock
which has just registered 7:01,
rendering him 1 minute late again
in the timekeeper's office upstairs
in some other building.
He almost collapses,
his energy level dropping
like an elevator with its cable cut
as he shakes his head and curses
and finally shuffles to his toolbox
where he fills out a timecard with a job number
to keep the men who walk around all day
carrying clipboards and writing down job numbers
happy.
Then he leans back in his leather swivel chair in
front of his machine,
putting his hands behind his head,
and stares up at the ceiling preparing to daydream
for an hour or two
before opening up a blueprint.

Tool Of The Trade

The machinists used their rollaway toolboxes like billboards,
plastering them with stickers and photos and posters
advertising their families,
their hobbies,
their opinions.
They filled them with booze and cigars and girlie magazines.
Parking them between their machines and the office,
they hid from supervisors
behind them.
Placards on their lids
threatened anyone who touched the rollaways
with death.

These machinists took their work seriously.

On Second Thought . . .

I know I'm not going to have a good week
when I come to work
Monday morning
and have to tear down the set-up
on my machine table,
throwing clamps and blocks and nuts and bolts
around as I curse
the stupidity and block-headedness
of that idiot on night shift who must have left me the set-up,
who ought to be fired who ought to
have been a janitor,
only to see
the machinist at the next machine
next to whom I work day in and day out
40 hours a week
keep his ear turned to me and then
walk over very slowly
with a very weird forced-looking smile on his face
to tell me
that actually as a matter of fact
he had come in for overtime on Saturday and been assigned
to my machine and worked all day to leave that set-up
I just demolished.

Sleepworking

At Goodstone Aircraft Company,
the ultra-slow turning of the machine cutters
and dials
and the dropping of chips from the sliced metal surfaces
of bomber parts
becomes hypnotic,
and everywhere machinists are nodding,
mouths falling open, heads jerking back,
as they snort and snore.

But over the years they have learned
how to keep themselves propped up
against the leather of their swivel chairs
without falling out of them,
and somehow
they are able to wake up just as their machines' cuts
are ending. They walk to the drinking fountain
and sprinkle ice-cold water on their heads,
or stand before fans
lifting their T-shirts up to their armpits,
knowing just how much to wake themselves up
so that they can reset their machines
for the next cuts.
Then they wiggle their asses
back into the impressions they have carved into
the leather of their chairs,
and get some more sleep.

Hard Worker

He would come by my machine
whenever I stared off into space
for a minute or two
to tell me that, "The company's not paying you
to daydream, goddamnit!"
frowning at me as he poked the stem of his pipe
at my Adam's apple,
then walking off in a self-righteous huff back to
his machine
where he wasted not a second
going back to work misinterpreting blueprints
and making inept set-ups
breaking cutters
and scrapping parts,
all the time keeping his jaws moving non-stop
as he griped and blamed everything
on engineers and supervisors
and company tooling.

Heartfelt

Machinists only really open up
and express their feelings to each other
when the right occasion arises—
like a machinist blowing up a razor-sharp cutter
in front of his face
or destroying an aircraft part
with $20,000 worth of labor
already put into it—
upon such an occasion
they will be there
to warmly cheer
and whistle approval and slap the man on the back
and laugh
in congratulation,
smiling with delight the same way they do
when a man is laid off
and they slap him on the back and chuckle and say,
"Short-timer, eh?"

Sinner

A machinist spends years on the same machine
surrounded by the same machinists at other machines
and sooner or later he is wandering up to the other machines
and confessing to the other machinists—
confessing that he didn't get laid last night
or that his wife is a feminist
or that he has "a friend" who calls
his wife "MA" and lives with her
even though she hasn't fucked him in years
and bosses every aspect of his life,
confesses that he likes David Bowie
or that his proctologist stuck a finger
up his asshole
or that he shakes his cock more than 3 times
after he pisses
or that his wife won't suck his cock.

Then he returns to his machine
and breathes a little easier for a few weeks or months,
until those relentless white floodlights
hanging from the ceiling of the building
get to him again.

Lingo

After years and years in machine shops,
machinists begin to talk less and less.
Instead, they begin to
tap their rubber or lead or ball-peen hammers
against their machines,
learning how to play their machines like steel drums.
They walk around with big sheets of sheet metal,
bending and buckling them
until they whirr and hum
like weird high-tech
guitar solos.
They line up cutter holders of varying diameters
and play them like organ pipes
by sticking the tips of their airguns into them
and blasting air through them,
or they blast air against the insides of their closed
fists and create kazoo-like sounds
by rubbing and opening and closing their fingers
and thumbs—

until occasionally, when they are really inspired,
they break out in vocals
to lead their own one-man bands—
the Italians singing opera,
the Mexicans mariachi,
and the bikers
heavy metal.

Every time it rains,
the machinists begin to glance up hopefully
at the roof above their heads and their machines,
staring fondly at the wet spots spreading
across the cork ceiling,
as around the building
raindrops begin to pour down in columns through
the leaky roof.
Around the shop
lucky machinists
jump up from their stools with glee
as the first drops hit their heads or their machines.
They whip open big sheets of plastic
as if they were bullfighter capes.
They dance with them,
grinning and hooting and tossing them
triumphantly over the tops of their machines,
turning to loudly snap shut the locks on their
toolboxes
and rub their hands together with glee,
having long ago ceased to gripe about Goodstone
Aircraft Company's refusal
to fix a roof
that provides them with such a perfect excuse
to go home early.

The Edge

The factory employs the desperate and the dangerous:
a man out of a mental hospital,
a man out of a prison,
a man out of the hills,
a man in a motorcycle gang,
a man who sits in front of his machine
sharpening his knife and throwing it
into the wooden platform under his feet,
a man who never talks,
a man who is covering his body with tattoos,
a man who is trying to become a writer.

Expertise

The new hire
wears perfectly ironed blue work
clothes,
keeps his hair perfectly combed,
organizes and files variously sized
C-clamps and U-clamps and heel blocks and spacers
in the cabinet beside his machine,
lines his tools out
on an immaculate white towel spread across his workbench
like a surgeon
ready to operate,
wearing magnifying glass lenses
in front of his eyes
as he sets up jobs on his machine table
according to the letter of the law
laid out by his 4-inch-thick
leather-bound *Machinist's Handbook*—
then scraps out part after part,
making them out-of-square,
undersize, backwards,
gouging them,
breaking cutters and cutting holes
into vises
and the machine table—
then immediately analyzing
with acute insight
and precisely correct terminology
the definitive reasons
for his errors.

Resigned

The new foreman was always on the verge of running,
seeming to point in 2 or 3 directions at once
as he told us what to do,
hurrying up and down the machine shop aisles
with his chest and chin out
and his arms swinging dramatically
like he was directing
some great life-saving effort that hadn't a second to lose,
telling us about how he could work 12 hours a day
7 days a week for a year
and always rush home after work to do things like
run up and down the front lawn
pushing a lawnmower,
still having plenty of energy left
after that.

We did all feel a little bad
as we slouched barely awake
in our leather swivel chairs
in front of our milling machines.

It was hard to sit by and watch someone
drive himself
to a heart attack.

A Bright Future

The veteran machinists who are competent
are constantly ridiculing Goodstone Aircraft Company.
They advise the new machinists
to get out
while they stilll can.

The veteran machinists who are incompetent
are proud of working at Goodstone Aircraft Company.
They strut about
and give the new machinists tips and advice
as if they were handing out priceless jewels.

"I'll show ya'" Carl says,
throwing levers and pumping handles with both hands,
moving his machine's table in and out
and right and left and up and down
as fast as he can,
as he marks dial calibrations and strips of tape,
creating path after path for a cutter to mill precise
surfaces onto a 1,000 lb. steel shank.
Soon the cutter is speeding across the shank,
tossing out arcs of orange and blue-hot steel chips.
Soon Carl crane-loads another shank onto the machine
and says, "You do it,"
and steps back
as the new man tries
to remember a few of the 32 steps
of the operation.
"WHAT'S THE MATTER, WEREN'T YOU WATCHING?"
"CAN'T YOU DO ANYTHING?"
"YOU'VE GOT A LOT OF NERVE WALKING IN HERE!"
Carl is screaming,
teeth bared, fists clenched, face crimson,
glaring at the new man
as if he were sure to be fired.

This is Carl's moment of glory,
the reason why he has the foreman feed him the new men
like chunks of raw meat.
This makes Carl's 25 miserable dead-end years at
his machine
worth something.

Cultural Exchange

Whenever the new Mexican machinist
has a spray can
of layout dye or lubricant or coolant
in his hand,
his Lead Man makes sure to walk up to him
and tell him
that he had better not be holding a can of spray paint
in order to spray graffiti all over something,
going into his guffaw laugh
and calling the machinist "ESE!"
and slipping his hand into his front pocket
and going into low-rider vato leg jiggling slouch,
punching back the brim of his cap
until it is almost standing straight up
and braying out,
"Wuuzzz APPening, maaaan?!"
over and over until he has forced
an adequate amount of laughter
out of the Mexican.

He wants to make sure to immediately break down
any racial tension
there might be between them.

A Learning Experience

Every now and then
a new guy at Goodstone Aircraft Company
questions the way things are done.
Raising his hand at shop meetings
and writing letters to vice presidents
month after month after month,
he protests the inadequate tooling
and unclear blueprints,
expresses outrage
at the stacks and stacks of redundant paperwork,
bewails the lack of morale
and proper management,
and gets nowhere,
until finally he is reduced to lurching about the shop
blurting out truths and shouting incredulities
to machinist after machinist,
still getting nowhere,
and looking more and more each day
like that guy trying to stop cars on the highway
in "Invasion Of The Body Snatchers."

Drowning

The new man
was 62 years old
and he jumped back and forth and darted
from one side of his mill table to the other
flapping his arms
and picking up and dropping nuts and bolts and clamps
as he played with various ways
of trying to clamp the aircraft part
down onto the table so that
he would be able to perform the very complex and touchy
machining operation
he had never done before,
his hands and arms jumping out and reaching
and flapping and moving
constantly
as if the fact that he was trying could somehow save him,
as the young Lead Man
refused to tell him one goddamned thing
and forbade any of the other machinists to tell him anything,
hoping to cause the firing
of this old man with the nerve
to take a job he wasn't 100% qualified for
just because he was desperate
for a job.

He never ran a milling machine before Goodstone Aircraft
Company hired him,
and now he walks around a brand new milling machine
with his head thrown back yelling
like a know-it-all,
changing the other machinists' set-ups
and hiding blueprints and manufacturing orders
and the manual for the new machine
in his toolbox,
fucking up parts and cutters and the machine table
as he flies into rages
about the stupidity of the manager
and grabs his cock and screams
that the manager can come down and suck it,
one day finally beating the shit out of a control panel
to the 1/2-million dollar new machine
with a lead hammer
and then clocking out early.

It does make you wonder just a bit
about that 9-hour aptitude and proficiency
and psychological
testing
personnel is putting all prospective employees
through.

Apprenticeship

The new man actually tried to work hard.

The veterans stared at him as if he were insane.
"Don't KILL the job!" they screamed.
They turned off his machine
and rolled his toolbox to the other end of the building.

The veterans were masters
at acting as if they were working.
They tapped parts
and studied indicators
and tightened and loosened and retightened bolts
hour after hour after hour,
accomplishing nothing.

Such consummate acting
was a skill that would take the new man years
to learn.

Occupational Hazard

He had begun screaming
broken sentences
at the top of his lungs,
jumping off the platform in front of his machine
over and over
as his machine ran.
His eyes darted about
as he cringed at the prospect
of his job creeping on and on and on
like Chinese water torture.

He had spent two years
learning the machine and the blueprints
and the machining operations
backwards and forwards,
until he could do his job in his sleep.

Now he was really going to have to start
earning his money.

Goodstone Aircraft Company
likes to show its employees videotapes
and our supervisor likes taking whatever tapes they
give him and shoving
them in and turning the VCR on and sitting back relaxed
indifferently letting us machinists learn
how engineers or expediters or assemblers or
supervisors should do their jobs,
letting us watch
crane operations or material handling or hazardous
substance situations
that we will almost certainly
never have anything to do with,
saying how it's good for us to understand and appreciate
the entire aircraft building operation,
but after shoving in a tape and letting us watch 15
minutes of instructions
telling us
where to put down "Wet Floor" signs and how
to wear rubber gloves and arrange cleansers
on carts and scrub floors
and toilet bowls,
our supervisor did have to admit
that we were probably wasting our time.

A company representative called us into the conference room
and handed "Ethical Decision Making" handbooks to us.
The representative told us that the company wanted
to help us be even more ethical
than we already were,
and we began reading the handbooks
that asked us to consider
involving ourselves in the personal lives
of our fellow employees
by reporting to our supervisors
such things as lying and problem drinking.

An hour later,
as we walked out the back door of the conference room
we made an immediate ethical decision
and threw the handbooks into the garbage can
as we filed past it.

Cleaning It Up

The "WE TIP" posters are up
all over building 61 with their
illustrations of pills and grass leaves
under big hypodermic needles
and their encouragement
of Goodstone Aircraft Company employees
to remain completely anonymous
as they call the DRUG HOTLINE number and report
anything that they consider might be suspicious or incriminating
behavior
in their fellow employees.

It's time to make this machine shop
a better place in which to work.

Formality

In the conference room
the company representative
had told us that it was criminal
to lie on our timecards
like we always did.
He had told us that we should avoid lying
by doing all of the things
he and the rest of us
knew were impossible to do
at Goodstone Aircraft Company.
Now he asked
if we understood all of the rules and regulations he had run
off in his
garbled spoken-much-too-fast impossible to sort out or remember
speech
and Jerry,
starting out of his snoring imitation
of deep sleep
and opening his eyes
said, "Oh, I think we UNDERSTAND, all right,"
with an amused smirk on his face,
and the representative nodded his head,
returned the smirk,
and said, "Good."

In the training classroom
the instructor tells us, "Supervisors tell me not
to teach you stuff 'cause if I teach you stuff
then you'll just fuck things up . . ."
but he goes on taking 8 hours each day
to teach us 10 minutes worth of information,
rambling and digressing and shuffling around
in front of his overhead projector
which he cleans with Coca-Cola from the vending
machine,
talking to us about his golf game
and his kids
and how the company buying the RL600 jet outside
bought it with windows
so that it could get the lower commercial
passenger plane price
and then knock the windows out and seal the fuselage
for mail delivery.
We sit back and smile and doze off
as worker after worker sticks his head in the door
asking if this is Sheet Metal class
or Shop Math class or bldg. 140,
the workers smiling knowing that it's routine
to spend the first day of a class
roaming buildings and aisles
with a sheet from your supervisor in your hand
giving you the wrong building and classroom
to go to.

Paperwork

Goodstone Aircraft Company has just come up with a new
system for reducing the number of scrapped parts.
It involves 8" x 11" Manila cards
covered with dozens of tiny little boxes
that must be filled in with blueprint dimensions
and part dimensions
and employee numbers.
Every machining operation on every part being made
must be numbered and kept track of
and inspected and approved
by inspectors and lead men and supervisors
who must rubber stamp appropriate boxes.

Hell, it's bound to work,
the machinists will be so busy filling out the cards
and getting rubber stamp approvals
that they won't have time to scrap as many parts.

Guts

The machinist
trained in the Goodstone Aircraft Company Public Speaking class
steps up in front of his fellow machinists
called in to sit around the 6' x 20' table
in the manager's Conference Room
and gives a talk
on the new part fabrication records
the machinists are to keep on Manila cards.
The machinist holds one of the cards up
and slaps and pokes it with a pencil,
stiff as a ram-rod
and sweating,
looking about to choke,
looking like
the manager has been jabbing his ass
with a cattle prod,
barking out his 800-word speech
on filling out the cards
at the top of his lungs,
shouting the words at the walls
as fast as possible
in red-faced, angry
desperation—

it sure was generous of Goodstone Aircraft Company
to enable this machinist to overcome
his stage fright.

It Slices, It Dices, It . . .

He says with this new miraculous program
we will have fun at work,
as much or more fun
at work as we have away from it,
as we become our own bosses and managers
by deciding how to make our shop run
with more and more efficiency and quality,
weeding out our fellow employees
who do not seem to want
to have fun
enough
by ostracizing them until they
leave
of their own free will—
we wouldn't want to make anyone do anything against his will
in this wonderful new system
where everyone has so much fun
doing exactly what he wants to do.

Auto-Didacts

We walk to the new Goodstone Aircraft Company auditorium
having been told we are to attend
a class on "material handling,"
but there is no instructor or podium
or overhead projector or VCR or screen,
so we 18 or so machinists
walk in
and fan out and take seats as far away from
each other as possible
in the empty 1,000 seat auditorium,
putting our arms and legs over the backs of
chairs and chuckling,
and after 10 minutes Bob yells out, "Hey Charlie get up there
on stage and sing us a song like you do at the nightclub!"
and Charlie yells back how Elvis Presley
had to go to special screenings
with bodyguards around him in empty 3 a.m. theatres
and now so does Michael Jackson.

Finally our Lead Man comes back from a phone
and admits that no one has any idea
where the class is really being given,
and we laugh and chortle as we rise
to leave, saying
how we've learned about as much in this class
as we have in the others
Goodstone Aircraft Company has given.

Refresher Course

Every time I started throwing
bolts and clamps and wrenches
around and breathing rapidly
like I was about to explode
with frustration and rage at trying to be efficient at some
fucked up, ass-backwards Goodstone Aircraft Company job,
my Lead Man
would come over to put his hand on my shoulder
and pat it and say very calmly,
"Let me buy you a cup of coffee, Fred,"
leading me away from my machine by pushing my shoulder
with his hand
until we were walking down the long long
aisle very SLOWLY
to the vending machine
where he pushed the quarter into the slot and bought me a cup
of hot coffee,
smiling and making small talk as we leaned against the machine
and wasted time,
then started to walk back very SLOWLY
watching all of the workers leaned back in leather chairs
with their feet up on workbenches
doing nothing
until the fact
that wasting time and money was no problem
at Goodstone Aircraft Company
had sunk into my head
again.

Promotion

He works feverishly
to keep that smile on his face,
constantly looks at pictures of Air Force generals
taped to the inside of his tool box lid,
straightening the little placard with his name on it
pinned to his shirt,
repositioning his cap with the Air Force wings
pinned to it
and spinning around in all directions
blasting chips away from his feet with his airgun
as he paces the platform in front of his machine,
trembling with furrowed brow
as he makes sure those pieces of blue paper toweling
he has tied around his machine handles
don't come off
and that piece of blue paper toweling
he has hanging out of his back pants pocket
doesn't fall out.

He just doesn't have quite enough energy left over
to keep from fucking up every job
he touches.

But he'll be alright.
Goodstone Aircraft Company has decided to put him into the
Planning Department
where everything is already
fucked up.

It's true that a job
sometimes sits in a box on the wrong rack or behind a cabinet
for weeks
lost and forgotten about by the
supervisors,
but the supervisors
immediately make up for it
upon finding the job,
slapping that red hottest-job-in-the-shop
AIRCRAFT ON LAND
sticker onto it
and running around in a pack
bumping into each other as they dart about
the machine they have placed the job on,
pointing and jabbering and nodding
as they scream about needing the job NOW
and ruin
whatever mental composure and readiness
the machinist may have had.

To check out a 2-3" micrometer
for a few minutes,
the machinist steps across the aisle
to the tool crib
where Gloria without looking up
will hand him a 2-3" micrometer
and a computer terminal print-out
that has his name, employee number,
job classification, pay rate
and senority date on it in triplicate,
as well as a 300-word tool loaning contract
which he must sign and date,
receiving his pink copy.

When the machinist steps back across the aisle
10 minutes later
to return the 2-3" micrometer to Gloria,
he hands in his pink copy
and she takes it and puts it on top of
the stack of folded computer paper
and rips all of the paper up and throws it into
the garbage can,
taking back the 2-3" micrometer
without looking up.

Less Than Zero

My Lead Man
brings me a new lead hammer,
picking up the barely-frayed lead hammer I have been using
and looking at it
and saying, "It's not safe,"
as he takes it away.
The fact that I know that my new lead hammer
will look like the one he has taken away
in just a few weeks
does not make me feel too secure,
especially since I know how rarely
Goodstone Aircraft Company usually replaces the hammers,
often making us use them for years,
the splintering shards of lead
flying up and stinging our faces
as we hammer until the hammerheads are
completely smashed and fall off
their handles.

Now I can't even say
they didn't warn me.

Togetherness

When a cutter Bob is using
suddenly balks and grabs steel
and explodes
with loud, nerve-wrenching rings and pops
that shoot out razor-sharp tool steel
fragments,
the machinists at the machines nearest the explosion
duck and then rise clutching their chests
with their tongues hanging out taking deep breaths
and staggering about on their platforms
as if they are having heart attacks,
staring at Bob and then grinning,
while the machinists further off on the machines
out of reach of flying steel
whistle and applaud
like spectators in an audience
who have just seen a good show
put on.

Goodstone Aircraft Company
was cited by OSHA
for failing to train and certify workers
who wore respirators
in the proper use and care of respirators.
So Goodstone solved the problem
by strictly refusing
to issue respirators
to workers who were untrained and uncertified
in the proper use and care of respirators.

Now no one can get a respirator.

The sliding steel door at the back of the building
is bent and dented and twisted off its track,
and lets big gusts of freezing morning air
blow into the building and upon Gus
at machine #495.
And whenever the towmotor drivers
towing aircraft skins on rolling racks
in and out of the building
use the door as a short-cut to walk outside,
they kick and shove it open
and leave it open
and Gus
immediatley marches over to kick and shove
as he slams it shut again
to keep from catching pneumonia,
until the door no longer slides at all
but opens and closes only with the most furious
lifting and shoving and kicking and slamming,
and Gus and the towmotor drivers
are shaking their fists and screaming their heads off
threatening to beat the shit out of each other,
and Frances
the old expediter,
puts down her clipboard to tell them
she is calling SAFETY
with a complaint requesting them to fix the door,
not because she actually believes
they might fix it
or even come out to look at it,
but because she hopes Gus and the towmotor drivers
can blame Safety
and thus avoid
killing each other.

Cover Your Ass

The new supervisor
stands before us and tells us
that all of our long-barreled 85 or 95 or 105 lbs.
of air pressure
air guns
are being immediately confiscated
to make sure that we
don't drop rivets
into them
and have guns.
In their place,
we are given 35 lbs. of air pressure
snub-nosed nozzles
that blow about as hard
as an old man
trying to blow out birthday candles,
while we wonder whose safety the new supervisor
is really concerned about,
ours or his.

Warning

I was looking at the lift
that opened
like an accordian made of thin steel beams with a metal
balcony on top
where welders stood
40 or 50 feet above the floor
while welding beams and crane bridges
and light fixtures,
and I was noticing how beaten and bent up
and twisted and old and grimy
the lift looked,
like it had been hit by a car
3 or 4 times,
when a man from Safety
walked by,
stopped, and motioning his head toward the lift,
said, "Yeah the cable snapped on one of those things the other
week and really fucked up a welder, collapsed his back—it's
okay if you check the thing but they don't check things
around here—you better be careful, you can really get hurt
really bad around here!"
Then he walked off looking righteous
and self-satisfied.

Once again,
Safety had done its job.

What The Hell

There is one
Hardinge chuck in building 88
and it is dysfunctional,
half of the handle broken off it and something jammed
or broken inside it.
The surface grinder operator comes over and starts taking
it apart again,
examining and tapping and liberally spraying
WD-40 lubricant
all over screws and rings and joints
as the machinists who long ago
resigned themselves
to using the big clumsy
Erickson chucks
laugh at him.
He laughs back at them,
and keeps on dismantling and fiddling and spraying,
and soon they are all laughing together,
each of them periodically coming out with the old stand-by,
"It all pays the same!"

On day shift,
Ralph
proves he has the most drive,
the most willingness to get the job done and the most ability
to get it done right,
the most skill and potential and the best attitude
in the entire machine shop.
So of course Goodstone Aircraft Company puts Ralph on the old
broken down machine at the far end of the building,
the big awkward obsolete machine
that leaks oil like a sieve—
its last 2 day shift operators
have fallen off it,
and its night shift operator
is drunk and stoned and uncommunicative and pissed off
every night trying to see how much he can fuck up
the machine and the jobs and the day shift operator.

And to think
Ralph had begun to wonder if Goodstone Aircraft Company
could offer him a challenge equal
to his exceptional talents.

The machinist is worried.

He has to keep positioning buckets in various places
under the table of his machine to catch
the oil that leaks out of his machine,
and each day he shovels oil-dry
absorbent
in a 4-inch-high wall
all around
the base of his machine
to soak up the rest
of the oil
that constantly seeps out and runs down the sides
of his machine.

If the oil doesn't start really pouring
out of the machine and creating a big oil slick
all over the floor,
he knows that Goodstone Aircraft Company will never even think
about fixing the machine.

Being Careful

The supervisor
comes over to tell me that I shouldn't
toss any of that oil-dry sawdust-like
absorbent
down across the concrete floor around my old milling machine
that leaks oil like a sieve
beause his bosses told him that some of the particles of
oil-dry MIGHT work their way into the machine
through coolant openings
and clog up the machine so that Maintenence
will have to take it apart again.
The supervisor looks pleased as I dump the tray full of oil-dry
back into the bin
and tip-toe slowly and lightly
across the oil and grease covered concrete floor
trying not to slip as I sidestep
puddles of oil
and return to my machine to step back up on the wooden platform
that is also covered with the slippery
filthy oil and grease.
The supervisor looks pleased
as I glance down
every time I have to take a step on the platform
to make sure that I don't slip and fall
and break my neck.

Wouldn't want that machine
to get clogged up.

The Wrecking Crew

At Goodstone Aircraft Company
the machinists put up with machines
that rattled, shook and lurched.
They put up with
worn-out machine brakes,
broken machine locks,
machine tables that moved only in one direction.
They moved buckets around
to catch the oil that poured out of the machines,
hammered on machine handles
and broke out in sweats hand-cranking machine worm screws
that should have turned automatically—
anything but call the maintenance department
and give them a chance to work on the machines.

The machines may have been falling apart,
but at least they weren't ruined.

The Routine

The maintenance man likes to ride his bike through the building
down the aisle
past Joe's machine
and point, as he slowly peddles and leans back leisurely,
at a ripped rubber cover or
broken off handle or
leaky hydraulic line
on Joe's machine
shouting over to Joe, "You should have that fixed!"
as Joe screams out, "Yeah so you wanna FIX it?"—
Joe knowing that the broken-off handle
or torn-up cover
or leaky hydraulic line
has been called into Maintenance a dozen times
and ignored.
Then the maintenance man likes to smile
and shout back at Joe,
"No, I'm just passin' through!"

Hell

They crouch down below the level
of their milling machine tables
to throw levers that set the tables moving
blocks of steel
into cutters,
jumping back from the machines
and running away in a crouch
as the cutters bite into the steel
with cutting edges
unevenly ground by the foreman,
cutters that often explode
into flying razor-sharp fragments
as they try to chew their way
through the blocks of steel—
the machinists peeking around the corners
of workbench backboards,
a good 10 or 15 feet away
from the machine tables
that shudder, hesitate, jump
as the smoking cutters make crunching ripping sounds
that send tremors through the machinists'
fingers and forearms
as the foreman
stands ready
and smiling
beside his trusty worn-down
50-year-old grinding wheel.

At first
the new computer milling machine
maintenance man
stands out like a sore thumb
as he really puts his all
into taking those computer machine terminals
and main control panels
apart and analyzing with master machine manuals
and sophisticated testing equipment
the precise reasons for anything less
than optimum machine performance,
going to management immediately
with fervent, earnest requests
for new components,
but soon
he is beginning to master
little by little some of the true Goodstone Aircraft Company
maintenance man's techniques and tricks,
like how to violently shove around and
grab and shake the shit out of
a computer machine terminal,
and how to open it up and randomly
and violently punch at wires and the backs of
components with a screwdriver handle,
and how to curse and frown and tell Goodstone to go fuck itself
as he hears in his head
all of the times Goodstone told him they couldn't afford
to buy the new components he needed.

They Built Them To Last In Those Days

The machinist hopes and prays
that his machine will finally break down
completely so that Maintenance will have to come
out and find what's wrong
and actually fix it,
but the machine keeps hanging on
by thin threads,
the machinist forced to run it
with its overhead ram pulled out to that one last spot
where the spindle will still turn
without tearing gears up,
as he chooses from the 5 or 6 spindle speeds
that still work
out of the original 20,
always having to pump the rapid travel handle
20 or 30 times
to get it to actually engage
and move the machine table,
wearing ear plugs and headphones
to withstand the noise of the machine head
knocking
as if rocks were being shot about inside it,
and constantly shoveling down oil dry
and moving buckets around
to catch the hydraulic oil
that pours out of the machine,
his blood pressure rising and his ulcer aching
as he forces himself
to keep from grabbing a 50 lb. lead hammer
like a baseball bat
and finishing his machine off.

Saved Again

My machine's head
is finally hanging by a thread
of a last bolt running through it,
the second bolt having finally stripped out
and sheared off just below the locknut
last night,
so Goodstone Aircraft Company
decides that yes the machine is definitely unsafe
and shouldn't be run,
doing me the service
of having Maintenance come up with 3 more bolts
to run through the head and lock with locknuts,
once again saving
this wonderful obsolete 60 year old machine
that shakes and runs only in high gear
and shears off
bolts.

Confidence

I walked in Monday morning
and saw that maintenance had put my machine back together
a month after taking it apart for repairs.
They had even covered the machine
with a fresh coat of green paint.
Of course I was skeptical,
knowing that Maintenance often did more damage
than repair—
they were known for taking our machines apart
with chisels and hammers and crowbars
and replacing bad parts with other bad parts.
"I sure hope this thing works right," I said to my foreman.
"It ought to," he snapped. "They painted it!"

Too Good To Be True

We couldn't believe it
when Goodstone Aircraft Company actually spent the money to
buy us 10 five-foot-high brand-new cabinets
with 8 three-foot-wide drawers each.
We immediately filled them
with cutters,
one grateful machinist piling stacks of heavy
stagger-toothed cutters
into the top drawer of his cabinet
until one day
he happily went to his new cabinet and tore open
a top drawer
and screamed and jumped
back
just in time
to avoid being crushed to death
by the cabinet
that tilted forward and fell over,
the face of its drawers driven
into the concrete machine shop floor
by 500 lbs. of weight—
Goodstone Aircraft Company had forgotten to have Maintenance
bolt the cabinets to the floor.

That we could believe.

Now We're Really Going To Have To Get Inventive

Goodstone Aircraft Company has finally found a satisfactory
way to fight back
at our misuse of its tooling—
our hammering on LOCK-RITE vise handles
when the expensive LOCK-RITE vises
are supposed to be hand-tightened,
our use of expensive, highly precision-ground
arbor spacers
under the ends of clamps we tighten down
with thousands of lbs. of torque,
our use of expensive,
highly-precision-ground microsurface-finished
parallel bars
as hammers,
our loosening of jammed chucks by pounding on them
with 50 lb. lead hammers
as hard as we can—
it's going to cut off all money for new tooling
and make sure we have to use
all this fucked up tooling
for years and years to come.

An hour to find a Hartford chuck,
half an hour to find a key for the Hartford chuck,
half an hour hammering on the chuck
because its rotation turns out to be jammed,
half an hour cursing Goodstone Aircraft Company,
an hour walking through 2 buildings
looking for another Hartford chuck,
an hour in a bathroom reading a sports page
to keep from going berserk,
another half an hour looking for a chuck.
An hour looking for 2 bolts
to lock the chuck you have finally found
onto your milling machine table.
15 minutes of throwing tools around,
kicking cabinets
and yelling obscenities
after you discover that the jaws will not close on the chuck
that you have bolted onto your milling machine table.
The remaining hour and 15 minutes spent
shuffling about 3 buildings
in a pretense of looking for another chuck
that you know you will never find,
that you no longer WANT to find,
that you no longer have the morale or energy
to do anything with
anyway.

Trapped

The punch presses
and automatic drill presses screaming and biting
through heat-treated steel,
the concrete floor
shuddering with the every-15-second pounding
of 2-ton drop hammers
and the rolling stomach-quaking heaving
of the 10-ton overhead bridge cranes
had worked on the steel mill veterans
until after 20 or 30 years
they always looked about to fight,
hunched over in their hard hats
with their fists clenched and held
up in the air,
thinking about their puny pensions
as the trembling
in their fingers
grew
until it took a very great effort
for them to sign their names.

The Source

The old man was deaf,
he just nodded no matter what you said,
but he was great with his thumb
he held it out in front of his eyes
and ran it up and down and left and right
like something magic
guiding his eyes
as he studied blueprints
and aircraft parts
with a precision and expertise everyone in the machine shop
admired,
and once he came over to my machine
with his thumb stuck out in front of his gut
thrusting it forward at something invisible
in front of him,
his eyes glowing with the magic
as he told me
how when he was a little kid
he and all his buddies
had used sticks in their hands
to push those big metal hoops
that came off kegs and barrels
up and down the sidewalks of New York
all day.

Solidarity

The workers
like to slam one heat-treated steel part against another
as they stack them in the steel bins.
After a worker executes a particularly loud ringing slam,
he will lift his face
to the tin ceiling 50 feet above
and begin hooting and screaming.
Other workers will join in
and the hooting and screaming
will grow louder and louder,
the workers encouraging and answering each other across the
steel mill
until every one of them is swept up
in a resounding chorus
that sends chills up the spines of the supervisors.

This is not the kind of cooperation
that the supervisors had in mind
when they talked to the workers
about working together for a better future.

The War

Whenever he could he hurled chunks
of steel
into the scrap metal bin—
banged them as hard as he could off the insides
of the steel corrugated walls,
timing it so that he
made our fingers jump
next to our razor-sharp milling machine cutters
spinning at 2000 rpm.
Or he made his punch press
shoot pieces
of razor sharp steel
at us,
shifting and positioning the steel he was punching parts out of,
aiming the flying shards of steel
at our eyes.

He walked with a limp
and whatever else Vietnam had given to him,
and we had long hair.

Unfair

She ran a drill press
and she was tough—
when the men machinists whistled and grabbed for
her ass or pussy,
she whistled and grabbed for
their asses and cocks,
the only difference being that the men
let her connect,
giggling and throwing their hands between their legs
a little too late.

The machinists
in the profile mill area
greet each other with loud resonant
"Hey BOY!"s,
while the boring mill section
likes to use a sharp
"Hey GUY!",
the computer mill section
yelling "Hey WALLY!"
at each other
even though no one in the building is named Wally.

That boring, mind-taxing task
of calling everyone by his correct name
is strictly for the supervisors.

The Aristocrats

The black machinists wore golden necklaces
and silky disco shirts
and dress pants
and panama hats.
They bent and contorted their bodies over their machines,
twisting around grimy, oily
handles and spindles and fixtures
without once touching their clothes
to machine or tool or part.
They were constantly blowing every inch of their clothes
down with their air guns,
to make sure that not one metal chip or speck of dirt
spoiled their look.

Radios in their pockets and headphone wires to their ears,
they disco danced up and down the wooden platforms
in front of their machines,
and disco danced across the aisles
to each other's machines,
slapping hands and grinning,
triumphant.

Spirit

The supervisor threatens to fire him
but Jesus goes on being Jesus
as his machine runs.
He recites Mass and imitates sirens and screams.
He sings mariachi songs
while the other machinists accompany him
with ball-peen hammer pings
and air gun wheezes
and bass notes on their vocal cords.
He calls people into the office
by imitating a voice over the loudspeaker,
rides the hand truck
like a scooter
around and around the workbenches and machines,
and says, "I sorry I sorry,"
grinning like the Cheshire cat
as the supervisor lifts the lead hammer
over Jesus' head
and threatens to kill him.

In the Goodstone Aircraft Company machine shop,
smirks are omnipresent
as i.d. badges,
as automatic to the machinists
as opening toolboxes
or cleaning the lenses of their safety glasses.
After a few years,
the machinists' faces are twitching with smirks
that have become tics,
until eventually their faces are lined
in the shapes of permanent smirks.
Anyone who doesn't smirk
is either a fool
or what is even worse,
uncorrupted.

It's Okay

For years they'd seen
the KKKs drawn and carved in the bathroom stalls
and heard the nigger jokes,
but when they began to see hangman's nooses
hanging from the beams
above their machines,
the black machinists
began to get excited and angry demanding
an end as they screamed in white machinists' faces
things like "Some of my relatives have died that way!"—
but Verl the old 39 year veteran
of the shop
didn't twitch a muscle or blink an eye
as he stayed stone-faced as ever
in the face of their screaming
and with utmost calm and reassurance
shrugged and said it was nothing it was just
that maybe the guys' sense of humor
went a little too far
sometimes.

Excretion

The workers
cover the bathroom stall walls
with messages
calling each other rat finks
who suck the cock
or lick the ass
of the boss.
They call each other faggots and niggers and kikes
and Buddaheads and donkeys.
They use knifetips to carve
KKKs and swastikas
and "Kill the Jews" into the wood of the stalls,
leaving unsigned threats about meeting each other
outside the plant gate—
while out on the shop floor
they smile at each other
and work together
cheerfully,
fully relieved by their stints
in the bathroom.

Strategy

He had a sign on his rollaway toolbox
telling everyone to bury him upside down
so they could kiss his ass.
He ran the machine
where they put the big 1/2-ton
wing carry-thru sections,
and his 35 years with Goodstone Aircraft Company
had rendered him an expert
at lifting and turning the wing carry-thru sections
with the crane
and running indicators up and down their sides all day,
then taking slow, thin cuts along the sides of the sections
until they were within .050" or so of being finished,
leaving the last, tension-packed
cuts for the night man
who would have to shoulder the stress
of the last do-or-die cuts
during which one false move
could scrap the sections out.
He went through one night shift man after another,
as they all sooner or later cracked
under the strain
until one night they were tearing up blueprints
or attacking the machine with a lead hammer
or throwing tools and cutters
out the back door onto the asphalt,
tearing their company i.d. badges off
and quitting,
unable to resist their one and only opportunity
to leave him with the do-or-die cut
for once.

The Enforcers

Whenever someone in the Goodstone Aircraft Company
machine shop loses control
enough to actually become somewhat
productive,
1 or 2 machinists
appear,
walking away from their machines
to come over
and stand near the machine of the offending
machinist,
lifting both their hands up
and forming fists one in front of the other
directly in front of their noses,
closing their fists until a hole the size of an invisible shaft
runs through both of them,
swiveling their fists in opposing directions
back and forth on this invisible shaft
in front of their noses,
signifying
the burrowing
of the machinist's brown nose up the ass
of supervision.

They want to make sure the machinist
doesn't mistake his aberrant behavior
for enthusiasm.

Trust

The guys all wore steel-toed shoes
and became expert
at stopping in the middle of their tending roaring
furnaces or the flaming oil of heat-treating tanks
to spin around on one leg
and kick backwards with their airborn leg
like a donkey,
the heel of their shoes
striking out behind their asses
in violent kickboxes
stopping just inches from the nuts
of fellow workers
they had spotted walking up behind them,
as their fellow workers never flinched,
but grinned and laughed and stuck out their hands
saying, "Give me 5!"—
reassured once again that they were working with someone
who was all right
after all.

Dills was our foreman
and he was working 84 hours a week.

Each day he would scream at us about working faster.

At 3:00 p.m. each day, after 12 hours of work,
Dills would race across the street
to THE RUNWAY
where he ate hot dogs and drank pitchers of beer
and screamed at the strippers.
He kept falling asleep in THE RUNWAY
with his jaw resting on his palm
as if he were still staring at the strippers.
He would finally leave at closing
and stagger back across the street
to a pot of coffee,
ready to start working again at 3:00 a.m.

After 2 weeks of this
Dills found himself face down on a table in THE RUNWAY,
unable to move his left arm or his left leg.

The paramedics took him away and Harry Green
won our gambling pool
by having come closest
to naming the date on which
Dills had his stroke.

Border War

The machinists stand at the lunch truck window
shoving bills at Marcela
as they tell her the wholesale price
of beef or coffee beans
has gone down so why has she raised her prices
and she yells back
"You cheap-ass gringo son of a bitch!"
and they joke about her degree from Tijuana Tech.
and she calls them faggots
in Spanish
and Wesley with his cowboy boots and steerhorn emblazoned
jacket
holds up the hot food line
for 5 minutes
again
as he rummages through every breakfast combo,
carnitas, beef, egg and chorizo,
and steak and potato
burrito
on the truck,
talking and then shouting about where the Hell is the
American food?

T.G.I.F.

After work each Friday
the workers celebrate the end of the work week
by rushing to their cars
and throwing open the doors,
denting the doors of the cars next to them,
the drivers of the dented cars
climbing out
and kicking dents into the offenders' doors.
The workers who make it out of the parking lot right away
rear-end
and sideswipe each other in the street,
and keep on going,
cursing and shaking fists and revving their engines
and jockeying for position
to get to the boulevard—
terrorizing and periodically running over
any workers foolish enough to forego cars
and attempt to cross the street on foot
to get to the buses.

They are walking out of the steel mill
after 10 hours of work,
pants smeared with rust,
fingers trembling
from the pounding of heavy machinery.
They wander out in front of traffic,
smiling and taking their time,
scanning the far horizon
with chins lifted,
as if to say, "Go ahead and hit me,"
as they stop traffic,
turning and tapping each other and laughing
in the middle of the street,
feeling the fear
of the people in the cars.

A Company Fence

Along the tunnel
that leads from the gate of Goodstone Aircraft Company down
under the boulevard and up to the employee parking lot across
the street,
3 x 5 foot sheets of formica
have been wire-bound along the chain-link fence
that separates the workers' walkway
from the one lane roadway that runs through the tunnel.
The formica sheets
do not lessen the nerve-shattering impact
of the towmotors and forklifts
running in low gear up the grades of the tunnel,
nor do they keep out the dizzying, nauseating exhaust fumes,
but they do give the workers the opportunity
to bang their swinging fists against them
as they march by
going home from work
in a 100-foot long single file line.
Everywhere up and down the line, the fists of laughing machinists
suddenly slam like sledgehammers
into the center of the formica sheets,
making them crack and boom and echo in the tunnel
as if though cranked up by amplifiers
next to the machinists' ears,
and all up and down the line
the raw-nerved machinists
are cringing and pulling their heads down toward their shoulders
and exploding
into uncontrollable jerks and spasms
as they fall victim to each other's
calculated pauses
and sudden, unexpected cracks and booms.

They are making the most of this one last chance
to fuck with each other's
nervous systems
as they leave their screaming machines behind.

Asleep

We machine the teeth of gears
and the cutting edges of drills.
We bore out cylinders,
turn pistons and rods,
thread screws and nuts and bolts.
We machine the dies
that stamp out pipes and seals and valves.

We are the engine, the driveshaft,
and the pump;
the wing and the wheel—

and yet we believe that we are powerless
as we sit in bars
and watch the President on television.

The Actor

Our old Lead Man
could be hard and tough
as they came,
throwing boxes of parts down on our workbenches and
barking out instructions and demands
as he glowered and scowled
and stuck his chest out
and let us know
that he didn't give a fuck how we felt about it,
but that eye twinkle
and smile and stroking of beard
and jiggling of belly
with laughter
were never far away,
and we all knew
that the only time he could really be himself
was once a year
on the day
a guy on a bicycle
pulled him around the machine shop on a flat
with boards made to look like a sleigh
as he wore the red and white suit
of Santa
and waved and yelled, "Merry Christmas!"

Support

He sat
with his eyes rolled back up into his head,
half falling out of my chair
as he told me that he had bitten the cheek of his boss
down at the company beach picnic,
his big gut full of a gallon of cheap white wine
heaving up and down as he tried to breathe and not throw up
and I said, "You're alright,"
and his wife sitting across from him said,
"No he's NOT alright he's fucked up it's OBVIOUS can't you
SEE it?"
and what could I say, he was my best friend
he'd invited me to his parties
where I'd
socialized for the first time in 4 years,
fitting right in
with the crazy ex-con
hippie biker dopers and
drunks
who had made me realize
that I wasn't insane
and shouldn't be put away.

The Idol

He organized our weekends,
piling us into his van
full of fishing poles and softball gear
and coolers full of beers.
He sat up tall with his chest out
in the driver's seat with his skipper's cap on
and his beard wet
with jug wine
as he drove us to piers or hills or beaches or parks,
chuckling fearlessly as he pretended to peer
at his van's radiator
while pissing all over freeway or highway shoulders
every 15 minutes,
chuckling with eyes full of wisdom as he precisely and
brilliantly analyzed our characters and identified our
problems
for us
around late night campfires,
and we
who had merely been in County Jails
or spent weekends in psyche wards for drug-induced
suicide attempts,
we listened with rapt attention to this man
who had
actually done long stretches
in Chino State Prison
and Camarillo State Mental Hospital.

Love Starved

He had a new wife and her 3 kids and another on the way
and he invited the 8 of us over
every weekend,
driving all of us and his family including his sidekick who
lived in the alley house behind him
to the recreation center
where he cannon-balled his 300 lb.
frame off the high dive
over and over
in front of us,
driving us all home
in his van to barbecue in front of us in his backyard
with his cooler full of beers
beside him on the dead grass,
telling us stories of helicopters and harpoons
and horizons from his swordfisherman days
and pulling out that newspaper photo of him standing beside
that record-breaking great white shark he'd caught
and passing it around again
as he talked about the movie "Jaws,"
doing acrobatic flips of chicken thighs
for us to watch,
his kids tugging at his pant cuffs
and his wife serving him
and all 12 of us people watching and hanging
on his every word
and still he looked off every 30 seconds or so wistfully
out toward the street
as if he wished the audience to arrive
any minute.

Carpe Diem

"Let's live LIFE!" he'd say,
lifting the gallon jug of wine and pouring the wine
into his mouth until the wine overflowed
into his beard and he licked it up
and looked
out his windshield as he drove
to the hills or the beach or the pier
on Friday mornings
after a week of graveyard shifts,
his eyes straining to stay alert and open
until as we all piled out of his van
at the beach or pier or hills
he was red-eyed walking half blacked-out
beginning to slump over and breathe heavily
but still forcing his eyes to stay open
as he walked around in circles trying to suck in
with his lungs and ears and nose and eyes and skin and brain
as much of the glorious taste of the work-week-ended freedom
as he could
before going to the van and passing out at midday and being
covered with a blanket
by his wife.

Uphill Fight

They were trying to ruin his life
he said,
the boss
who fired him just because he missed his 7th
Monday in a row,
the girlfriend
who left him just because he kept demanding
blowjobs all the time,
those cops who kept stopping him
just because he had long hair and drove a hippie van
with curtains
and liked to stomp on the gas pedal a little
when he was drunk,
and those asshole voters and politicians
who kept inacting new drunk driving laws
that made him do longer and longer stretches
in County Jail.

Pretty soon they were going to make it
so even a guy as smart as him
couldn't keep his shit together.

Accepting His Award

The more he drank
and smoked dope and spent all day and night
watching television
as his unemployment claim ran out,
the more he talked
about a job he'd had a long time ago
at T&S Containers,
about how he had worked there 6 years
and really paid his dues doing all that
mindless dehumanizing assembly line heavy lifting
work,
never missing days or fucking up
like he always did now after just a week or 2
at some place that
hired him,
and soon
after more and more intense drinking and dope smoking sessions,
he wasn't even looking for work anymore,
he was only getting fucked up and watching T.V. and
just finally flat-out
doing what he'd deserved ever since
he'd put in those 6
grueling sweaty humiliating years of
sterling attendance and performance at T&S Containers—
resting on his laurels.

Celebration

When he got the $2,000 settlement from the shipyards
for falling through a ship's hatch while working,
he had a week long party.
He walked around
balancing 6-inch high
mountains of cocaine
on a big round mirror,
getting all of his friends high,
listening for police helicopters
and locking his front door
whenever he heard one,
laughing and giggling and grinning
as he thought about his sister and her husband,
the Jesus freaks in Oregon,
whom he was sure would take him in
when he told them he could no longer make the rent
or find a job.

The Lid

"I'm legally insane," he would say
at various times,
some times as an emotionless straight statement of fact
and warning
when he walked into a party,
other times meekly and with wonder and fear in his voice
to his best friend,
and still other times loudly, boisterously
and followed by an ironic, defiant laugh
as he led another 3-van 4-motorcycle
camping expedition
into the hills—
it was mostly to himself
that he was talking,
reminding himself because he had to—
it was the only thing that really seemed to keep him sane.

Ordeal

Those long Saturday afternoons
hanging onto the phone for hours and hours
as he told me
about being tortured in the mental hospital,
about sleeping in parks
and roaming bars at Happy Hour
stealing olives out of cocktail glasses,
about Jesus
and his motorcycle
that were his only friends,
and I admitted to him
that I was afraid to go outside on weekends
yet never missed a day of work,
that I had wanted to be dead for 4 years
and yet still was terrified
of losing my job,
that I wore a silver crucifix around my neck
and yet believed
in nothing.

Captive Audience

Every day our manager
circled and circled our apartment building,
shouting to anyone who came outside
about all the times
he'd been around the world.
The alcoholic in the apartment behind me ate less and less
and drank more and more,
and I stuck my head in the oven
and set my mattress on fire,
and the old lady in the apartment in front of me
kept calling the paramedics
because she couldn't breathe,
as the manager kept circling the building,
each day shouting a little louder
about Japan and Germany
and the Fiji islands
and . . .

The Best Days Of My Life

Working at the steel mill
all day,
burning my fingers on the hot crane chains
and searing the insides of my nostrils
at the mouths of furnaces,
smiling and staggering
with hangover
until I drove home
to flop about in my broken-down chair
in my depressing-as-possible apartment,
downing 6-pack after 6-pack
listening to
Hank Williams songs
of lonesomeness and desperation,
leaning back to burn the back of my chair
against my wall heater,
lighting ovensfull of gas fumes,
burning my mattresses
and throwing open windows and running out
under 2-foot-thick clouds of smoke—
I wanted to walk as far out on that limb of death
as possible
and dance about on it
while I was still in my prime.

Moral Indignation

As I ran my machine
Monday morning
they backed away
and looked at me out of the corners of their eyes
when they thought I wasn't looking
and shook their heads as they spread the word
that I had burned up my mattress
2 days after blowing up
an oven full of gas in my face,
never speaking to me except to say things like, "I won't be
writing any letters home to YOU!"—
angry at the sight
of my moustache and eyebrows that were half burned off
and white with ash,
their faces, their noses drawing back
whenever they had to come
within a 10' radius of me,
disgusted, furious
at the bandage
on the red swollen skin
of the inside of my right arm,
righteous
with their bibles and crosses
in their pockets
and toolboxes.

The Pressure's Off

My fellow workers
are passing around the article in the paper about my being
a poet of the working class,
and to my surprise are delighted,
coming up behind me to applaud loudly
behind me as I munch on a sandwich at break,
shaking my hand proudly
around the big circular sink where we all wash up,
whistling the melody to "Hollywood" when I am around
and calling me "The Movie Star"—

I guess it must be a hell of a relief
to know for sure
I'm not the narc
they thought I might have been.

A Threat

My fellow workers and I
operate machines that cut steel blocks.

As the machines cut the steel,
my fellow workers like to stare and laugh at each other.
They are ready to piss on each other's graves.

They fear me.
They call me crazy.
They don't like the poetry I read.
They don't like the paintings I have hung
on the board behind my machine.
They look at me
like they want to cut my balls off.

Tomorrow I think I will start bringing roses to work.
Each day I will stand a rose in a jar of water
on the workbench behind my machine.
I want to really terrify my fellow workers
this time.

Warning

In his office
the steel mill manager
asked me what I was doing working in a steel mill
and told me
about the worker
he had sent to a psychiatrist.
The manager grew livid,
stroked the big jagged scar across his forehead
and told me he had wanted to be a doctor
before WWII had destroyed his dream,
then asked me again
what I really wanted to do
as I sat hungover and sleepless and shaking
and determined not to tell him I wanted to be a
writer.
The pounding of the drop hammers and punch presses
roared through the steel mill wall
and he told me that a person who was going insane
usually had no idea it was happening.

Scapegoat

In the machine shop,
dayshift and nightshift always blamed
bad parts and slow production
on each other.

To dayshift,
nightshift was full of lazy, incompetent assholes
who depended on dayshift
to carry their load,
while to nightshift
it was the other way around.

The delusion did not last forever,
however.

When a man had to switch shifts,
he was finally forced to see
the error of his thinking:
those lazy, incompetent assholes
on his former shift
had duped him.

Help

I knew it was
the Korean black belt ex-soldier
who ran my machine on night shift
and was mad at me for working too fast,
who had left a model
of a hand grenade
on top of my toolbox
for me to find in the morning,
and it was a model of absolute verisimilitude
made out of modeling clay we used to add weight
to aircraft parts
and complete with a 2" long 1/4" in diameter
steel pin through its cap,
and I immediately showed it to my supervisor
who grabbed it and studied it and said,
"Thanks, we've been looking for people who've been doing this
kind of stuff," and walked off with it.

Which didn't make me feel much better,
considering how many times I'd shown the supervisor
"stuff" like
the trails of red layout dye
dripped across my workbench
like blood,
and the drawings of blood-dripping bayonets
taped to my machine head.

Swinging Into Action

Suddenly I notice that
the night shift man
has forgotten to tighten the locknuts
on the head of my machine,
leaving it any minute
liable to shake loose
and come spinning sliding and crashing
its 300 lb. weight
down upon me as I work trapped
between my machine and the workbench behind me,
so I tell my supervisor
who calls Maintenance to somehow
hammer the locknut bolts into position
on the teetering head,
but Maintenence tells me
it's the operator's job and that
they can't do it,
so my supervisor calls Safety
and they come to tell me
that actually the head should have been taken completely off
in accordance with safety procedures
and leave,
as the layout man eating an apple
15 feet to my right
smiles and chuckles and shakes his head
and says
how he knows how to get things done
but the only trouble is
he's not supervisor.

Status

The Lead Men
at Goodstone Aircraft Company
relish their yawns, they wait for them
as they walk about the aisles
all night with nothing to do,
they turn them into long-as-possible
loud-as-possible
hoots
or whistles that hang in the air for 15 or 20 seconds
like dropping bombs,
until their mouths slam shut and they shake their heads
and breathe deeply forcing their eyes
to stay open,
then smile and raise their noses high in the air
like peacocks
who have just displayed their tail feathers.

Uptight

Bob tightens the nuts
down onto the clamps.
He is grunting and grimacing,
his biceps straining
and his back nearly wrenching out
as he turns red and tugs on a 2-foot-long crescent wrench,
digging his boot heels into the concrete floor.
He gets out a 4-foot-long section of steel pipe
and slips it over the crescent wrench,
grabbing the pipe as if it were an oar,
leaning back,
giving 4 final tugs
that make the nuts and bolts creak
as if they are about to snap.

The slab of aluminum he must cut is now anchored
to the machine table with more than twice the torque
required to keep extremely hard heat-treated
tool steel
from moving under the force of cutting.

Bob doesn't want that son-of-a-bitch
on night shift
to think that he can tighten nuts
tighter than Bob can.

On Top Of Things

The operator
of the computer mill with the 30' high vertical beds
had lowered his cage to ground level
and gotten out of it
to get a coffee,
but the machine hadn't given him any coffee and it also
wouldn't give him his quarter back
so he climbed back into his cage
and rode it on its tracks 15' up
the face of the mill bed to take a
50 lb. 12" C-clamp
off of a set-up and bring it back down
and swing it
like a baseball bat
again and again
into the face of the coffee machine,
denting the machine and rocking it and caving it in,
sweating and shaking and out of control
with quarter-maddened fury.

He'd be God-damned
if that coffee machine would make a fool of him.

The Loser

Nothing inspired him like a cutter holder
that wouldn't budge.
His toes would dig in
to the leather of his steel-toed boots
as his hand and forearm throbbed,
his fingers turning white
as they strangled the hammer handle;
he would strike again and again,
blinking
as if he were about to cry,
unable to stop hammering
long after there was any chance
of it doing any good;
hammering at the fact
that his hammering was useless,
at the fact that he was there
hammering himself
into exhaustion.

Trademark Of Quality

I have traded in my
Goodstone Aircraft Company attendance competition certificate
at the Company store
for a toolbox, a lunch pail,
a photo album and a set of
carving knives,
and two days later
I have had to hammer half-inch deep dents
into my toolbox with a steel punch
in order to get the drawers
to open,
learned how to force shut my lunch pail
with its ill-fitting latches,
and have found that our photo album
will not close
and that the extra leaves we bought for it
have hole patterns
that will not let them fit into the album's spiral binding,
and that
our carving knives
have unfinished wooden handles
that have already become water-logged.

I guess Goodstone Aircraft Company wants to make sure
we won't forget who gave us
the stuff.

The Inspection

Whenever a good-looking secretary walks down the aisle at
Goodstone Aircraft Company,
the machinists make a point of staring at her
from the moment they spot her.
They move around their machines
to keep her tits and ass and thighs
in view,
making sure that it is obvious
they are watching her.
They drift away from their machines,
sticking their necks out into the aisle
to keep her in view
until she is out the door of the building.
Then they let out with shrill whistles,
shaking their heads and hands
and going limp all over as if they were about to collapse,
making sure that everyone knows
how much their lustful minds sucked in
every inch of every curve on her body,
competing with each other
to see who
can stagger and whistle and maintain
their open-mouthed blank-eyed look
the longest,
glancing about at each other
to take stock of the results.
Finally, when it is safe to quit whistling and moaning
tributes to her body,
they return to their machines,
reassured that they have once again passed
the test.

If they want to take a holder or parallel bar or clamp
from under the workbench of another machinist
who is obviously not using the parallel or holder or clamp,
the thin-skinned machinists will hold the tool up
in front of the other machinist's face
and humbly and fearfully beg with a gesture of their heads
and eyes
to use it,
as if to take it without asking
would sentence them to violent death,
just as they make sure
never to nick or in any way mark or dirty
or move by even half an inch
another machinist's rollaway toolbox,
just as they immediately say
"Excuse me!" or "I'm sorry!"
if they happen to knock against another machinist
with their elbows
as they move about in the tight quarters
around and between the machines—
especially if they are some of those big tough thin-skinned
biker machinists with gang patches
on their leather jackets.

Naturals

Bikers make great machinists.
In machine shops
they can stink and swear
and strut
about in front of their machines
as if on stage,
hundreds of glaring floodlights
above their heads and the heads
of the 20 or 30 other machinists
who must watch them
40 hours a week.
Machine oil dripping from their fingers,
they pull and hammer
and visegrip steel for 8 hours
until steel explodes into speed
between their legs
and they ride
down asphalt to bars
where they can parade about
and fill up with beer
to keep themselves running smoothly.

His flesh was bloated and blood red.
He kept a high-velocity fan
blowing full blast on himself summer and winter,
and he made the veins in his neck and temples stand out
like worms
as he shouted at the men at the machines around him
about having been in every jail in Southern California,
about whiskey and beer
and his 6 drunk driving arrests.
Each week there was a new
skull or tombstone or vulture
from "The Tattoo Artistry Of Stan Dark"
on his arm or belly or hand,
and he said he'd never done better work
than at that shop in Lynwood
where they'd let him keep a bottle
right there in front of himself
on his milling machine table.

Connoisseurs

Collection boxes and cards were always coming around
for the vigilante machinists
who were dead or in the hospital
with gunshot or knife wounds,
and sometimes the police came right into the machine
shop
and walked a vigilante machinist out
in handcuffs
under suspicion of murder.
The vigilante machinists kept guns in their cars
and their toolboxes,
and were always throwing their buck-knives into the
wooden platforms under their feet.
Their hero
was the lucky son-of-a-bitch who got to pull the
switch to the electric chair
and at the end of the shift
they liked to lick their lips and talk to each other
about going to "The Morgue" to "get a couple
of cold ones."

Mack Truck

Armstrong's 30-foot-long bedmill
was the biggest machine in the building
and he liked to
march his 6'6" 230 lb. frame
around it,
wearing his khaki pants and shirt and his
khaki Marine-style cap,
sticking his chest out and going, "BEEP! BEEP!"
whenever he felt especially good,
"BEEP! BEEP!"ing his way
over to the smaller machines around him,
looking down
at the operators of the smaller machines
and winking
and lifting his nose in the air as he motioned
with his head toward their machines
and said,
"Kind of like running a sewing machine, isn't it?"

He was 4'5" tall
and threw a steel-mesh step down in front of his
machine, standing
on it so that he could reach handles and drawbars
and see the parts he cut
on his machine table,
and when he wasn't standing on his step
he liked to look up at the 6'2" mill operator from
the next machine
and tell him with a booming voice
that he could do the work the 6'2" operator
had just taken all day to do
in one hour,
puffing his chest out and swaggering
and snorting with contempt and conceit
as he threw clamps and set-up blocks
around,
as the 6'2" mill operator looked down at him
furious at how unfair it would be to hit
a man
4'5" tall.

They liked to sneak up behind each other
and goose each other
with yardsticks and hammer handles and broom handles
seeing how far they could make each other jump.
They liked to talk about
County Jail and wolf tickets and ripped assholes.
They liked to climb over each other
to get a good view of the secretary
when she swayed her ass up and down the aisle.
They liked to talk about the blow jobs she
was giving the company president in his office
during lunch.
They liked to shout in deep
booming voices about NFL games,
sticking their chests out and strutting about
bragging about how much they could bench-press,
poking each other in the chest
and pulling each other's beards
as they called each other niggers
and mex's and buddaheads.

They were true buddies.

Bad Apples

Once again,
Lionel walks
around the bathroom dividing wall to the side
with the long trough urinal where machinists
are pissing and pulls out his cock and says,
"Is this where all the dicks hang out?"—
laughing and stepping back from the trough
to let go with an arcing 3-foot-long
stream of piss as he tells
dirty jokes and all the men pissing into the trough
turn red and hurry to zip up,
wishing they had gone to one of the stalls
around the other side
to piss,
although that wasn't much better what with
Earl sitting down in there endlessly
and loudly and resonantly humming
"Swing Low Sweet Chariot"
again.

The pussy men
buried their faces in the pages
of pussy magazines.
They had pussy shots on their keychains
and the insides of their toolbox lids.
They talked about pussy constantly,
about all of the pussy they had fucked,
and all of the ways they had fucked it.

The gun men
puffed on long cigars
and read gun magazines.
They wore gunshop T-shirts
and covered their toolboxes
with gun photos and NRA stickers.
They marched around their work areas
keeping their machines spotless by blasting them with
air guns they had fitted with 3-foot-long barrels.

No one survived
in that machine shop
without guns or pussy.

Our Lead Man liked avocados
and he liked to walk around the shop holding 2
between his legs
like huge green balls,
he was always telling the secretary
to hide one of her jelly beans anywhere on her body
he'd find it with his tongue,
he stuffed
big jelly donuts
into his mouth and licked his fingers
and smacked his lips
as he walked about the shop
sticking his beer belly out as far as possible
and shoving people aside with it
as he made his way
from machine to machine,
looking at our fishing and pussy
magazines
and talking about things like how that big gaping cunt there
must have been pulled in
on a 500 lb. line.

Covered

Larry was 6'5" with broad powerful
chest and shoulders and he wore
skimpy tanktops and had that photo
on the inside of his toolbox that made it look
like he was holding a V-8 engine and block
over his head in his 2 hands.
Larry liked to talk
about the times he'd stood before judges
on felonious assault charges,
and every now and then
we'd look over to where he worked
and see him ripping up blueprints and throwing the pieces
back over his shoulders,
breaking off cutters out of machine holders
with lead hammers
and picking up big clamps and steel blocks and bolts
and hurling them all out the back door
onto the asphalt outside,
knowing that the Lead Man wouldn't say anything
because the Lead Man had made sure Larry had that machine
all by itself back in the corner by the door—
Larry was the Lead Man's
personal bodyguard.

Unsolved Case

His macho
exhibiting of his musculature
in the shop,
regular stretching exercises in which
he swung his arms out
and then brought them in to cross them in front of his chest
flexing pectorals
and biceps and triceps
and then strutted about his grinding machine
tall and square-shouldered,
made even more odd
his pornographic stories
from the point of view of a woman he kept leaving
in the workbench drawers
and the way
he was always asking the other machinists if they liked bananas,
laughing after he asked them
and then walking off
whistling the melody
to "Yellow Submarine."

The Stud

He had worked out at Gold's Gym
until he could bench-press 450 pounds.

He walked around the machine shop
waving a 50-pound lead hammer above his head
with one hand,
and his hammer blows
echoed off the machine shop walls
like gunshots.

Then he started talking
about how much he liked to fuck
his boyfriend.

For the first time in the machine shop's 20-year history,
no one was telling any faggot jokes.

Service

The tool crib attendant
looks hopelessly and angrily
through cabinet drawer after cabinet drawer
in search of micrometers and cutters and gauges
the machinists ask for.
She is unprepared and unknowledgeable
and usually unable to find anything,
but she wears the tightest jeans and lowest-cut
blouses possible,
and bends over to give the best possible views
of her beautiful ass and tits
to the machinists
waiting at the tool crib gate.
She scowls and slams shut the drawers,
usually empty-handed as she walks back to the gate,
shaking her head smugly
as if she had already given the machinists more
than they deserved.

Which is usually fine with the machinists
who usually don't really need what they've asked for
anyway.

The machinist who tried to kill himself
because he couldn't stop crying like a girl
when he was on PCP;
the machinist holding up the pussy magazine
in front of his face
to be sure everyone knows he's staring at it;
the machinist in a constant rage
because his wife won't give him a blowjob;
the machinist telling everyone how much he hates
the queers on the 2nd tier of the L.A. County Jail;
the machinist who walks around with a tape measure
pulled out to 12 or 15 inches
and held in front of his fly;
the machinist who wears a hat saying "U.S. Male"
and smokes big cigars
and weightlifts steel bars and arbors
while his machine runs:

being a man in a machine shop
is not easy.

Entitled

The 20 or 30 years in the machine shop
become too much for some workers.
After weeks and weeks of being absent from work,
one is found sprawled across a beach
staring open-mouthed up at the sky.
Another comes out of the machine shop bathroom
and throws a cupful of shit
onto the white shirt of his supervisor,
while another suddenly begins being chauffeured
to work in a limousine,
wearing a 3-piece suit
and talking about the million dollar ideas
he is going to talk to the company president about.

These workers figure they've earned the right
to go crazy.

The supervisor hovers about,
periodically shaking Rick
and screaming "Earth to Rick! Earth to Rick!"
into his ear.
Rick moves and laughs and flexes his fingers
and follows the path of his machine's cut
for a minute or two,
until he stops halfway through a swivel
in his leather chair
and his eyes are suddenly glazed again
and he has gone back
to that place no one else knows anything about,
as he sits transfixed and a million miles away,
his machine turning automatically
through a 40- or 50- or 60-minute cut,
the supervisor hovering and shaking him and screaming,
glad to take care of someone
with such an exceptional talent
for never getting bored,
no matter how monotonous and mindless
a job gets.

Recovery

He said his intense concern
and involvement with doing his job right
had worked him into apoplectic states
and given him high blood pressure,
so now
he didn't give a fuck
and was healthy,
shrugging off the parts he gouged and shattered,
his blood pressure down
as he waltzed about
and forgot to tighten
the locknuts
on his machine's head,
whistling
as the 300 lb. head
balanced unbolted
5 feet above him,
ready to come bouncing down on him
where he stood trapped
between the machine and the workbench,
chuckling
and looking off into space
relaxed
as he could be.

Happy

The manager of the machine shop wants me to be HAPPY.
HAPPY as I wrestle
60-pound jackhammer cylinders
up onto my milling machine table
faster and faster.
HAPPY as the manager extends overtime another hour
and tells me I have to work the weekend.
A HAPPY smile
and a nod
when the manager asks me if I am HAPPY.
I am so HAPPY I can hardly stand it.

The manager says life is too short to be unhappy,
and I can feel my life
getting SHORTER and HAPPIER
every day.

God's Work

Roberto was an accident-prone machinist
who prayed to Jesus and the Virgin Mary
and ran mill tables and parts and fixtures
into cutter after cutter.

Roberto was never scratched
as the cutters exploded in front of him
like hand grenades,
sending countless razor-sharp slivers
flying past his head and shoulders
toward the surrounding machinists
who ducked and collapsed under their workbenches.

The machinists were beginning to believe
that Roberto was blessed by God,
and Roberto's exploding cutters
were converting more of the machinists to Christianity
than the T.V. evangelists ever would.

"HOW TO GO TO CONFESSION"
the pamphlet on the inside of his toolbox
said,
and he kept glancing at his right hand
as he said his wife was Catholic and he'd
converted when he married her
but he couldn't
quite make it to confession
yet Vatican 2 would be okay you just
sat there in a chair face to face with the priest
who sat in a chair too
but that Vatican 1
that sitting in a booth behind a curtain
it spooked him
he said
glancing at his right hand again,
it made him feel like he was in 8th grade
again
that's why his wife had got him the "HOW TO GO TO
CONFESSION" pamphlet,
the only thing was he just couldn't seem to get around
to reading it,
he was going to end up like Al
that guy over on machine #702
the guy who never got upset no matter what you said
the guy who was on medication.

On His 22nd Birthday

He ate with us
on the plastic bench
outside the steel mill,
biting off chunks of a cheese sandwich
and swallowing them
bitterly,
as if each mouthful that entered his stomach
were a defeat
as he scowled out of the corners of his eyes
at the tin corrugated wall of the steel mill
and talked
about how near death he'd been,
how pale and thin and malnourished
and how much he'd scared those doctors,
his shoulders squaring and rising
with pride
as he set his thumb against the upper front teeth
of his dentures
and shoved them back,
then took his thumb out of his mouth and ran it
through the gray hair
curling down to his shoulders,
until he slumped again
and fell silent,
staring at that last chunk
of cheese and mayo and Wonder Bread
in his fingers
angrily
for a long time
before he ate it.

The Hunter

Jackson
had a gun in his toolbox.
He read gun magazines
religiously
during breaks and lunch
and while his machine ran through automatic cuts,
and he always took dead aim with an invisible rifle
in his hands
at birds when they flew into the 60 foot tall
building and lit on overhead beams,
and whenever he was mad at
a blueprint or a part or a boss
or a fellow worker
he raised his right arm and
closed his fist and raised his thumb straight up
and stuck out his index finger like the barrel of a gun
and pointed it at the offender,
and he always spent the last half hour
of his shift continuously
running out to the fence outside to spy through it at the
parking lot looking for whichever night shift man was going
to park next to his car,
looking to see if he could catch him putting a nick or a dent
into his car with his door,
peering through the chain link fence like he was drawing a bead
on some animal
he could taste.

Return to: Sue Stathers, Gender Studies, University of Hull, HU6 7RX

I ~~will~~/will not attend the Gender Studies finalists' meal.

Name ...Elaine Cassidy.......

Telephone Number ...846.895.......

I would like a vegetarian/chicken starter (soup)

I would like a vegetarian/chicken/prawn main course

Please delete as appropriate

THE QUEEN's
ANNIVERSARY PRIZES
FOR HIGHER AND FURTHER EDUCATION

1996

Good In A Crisis

Rod
was grim
all day at his machine throwing tools around and scowling
and smacking the head of his rubber hammer
down onto his sheet metal workbench,
looking wounded and vindictive
and angry,
except
when his machine spindle
slipped and tore up gears
with ear-splitting grinding and slapping
or his cutter grabbed and bit into the metal wall
of a part to bend and snap set-up bolts
and chew and tear and ruin the part
and explode
into flying shrapnel,
then
he beamed and burst into irrepressible
grins and threw his head back
laughing
until he had to steady himself with his hand
against the edge of his workbench
to keep from rolling around on the floor
in hysterics.

He was a big black machinist
and he brooded
constantly
about how the government made us work 40 hours a week
it kept us from knowing
what was going on it kept us from finding out
about things how could we know
what was really going on if we had to work 40 hours
a week,
brooding about it constantly until he couldn't stand it any more
and for a few moments
he'd stop shaking his head
and talking about the government
and make a big imaginary plate with his spread
thumbs and index fingers
under his chin
and open his eyes wide and look down at it
and inhale as if he could smell the aromas
as he talked
about mashed potatoes
and gravy and peas and pot roast,
happy for a little while.

Truth Serum

He said
the grass he always smoked right before work and during
lunch break
made him get into his work more,
and you could see it
in his transfixed eyes
and silent meticulous handling
of aircraft parts and machine controls
as he performed his work with an almost
reverential awe,
but when he took acid
that one time
it wasn't quite the same as he found himself
unable to do anything
but wander to the machines
of machinists he hoped he could confide in
to tell them he was on acid.

Mel Took Acid At Work

3 hours later,
Mel began circling his machine with bucket and brush,
cleaning every inch of his machine
again and again,
until he dropped his bucket and brush
and began trotting around his machine.
He trotted faster and faster around his machine
until he shot off down the aisle,
his arms and legs pumping
as he ran out the door of the machine shop
and headed for his car.

Victorious

The janitor's body is thin and stooped
over with the tens of thousands of times
he has stooped over
to grab chip bins and hoist and empty them
into dumpsters
he pulls with his scooter
as he tours the buildings,
his body is twisted to the side with the way he leans
and twists out of his scooter grabbing
trashcans off of floors beside workbenches,
his body is stooped and twisted and shaky
with exhaustion
and 60 years,
but yet
on his face lined with the scowls and frowns
supervisors have put there
are constantly breaking out
shit-eating grins of delight
that make his eyes light up
as if something inside him
is growing stronger
all the time.

Fringe Benefit

The janitor towed lines of dumpsters
up and down the machine shop aisles,
across the loose steel plates
that covered the scrap-metal conveyor belts
under the aisles.

The janitor nodded with booze as he drove,
tipping forward and sideways
in the towmotor seat,
leaning like he was about to fall out,
his eyes red and barely open.

But he made the machine shop explode
with the pops and bangs and cracks
of the steel dumpsters jarring and bouncing
across the steel plates
as he drove the towmotor FAST
down the aisles.

Not only did this keep him awake,
it helped ruin the already raw nerves
of the machine shop supervisors.

Every job has its rewards.

Relief

The machinist at the machine next to me
was always coming around
sticking his face between me and the work I was trying
to do to let me know how HE would do the job,
distracting and confusing and enraging me
with his useless and incompetent suggestions
until I could barely perform the work I was doing.

But I finally lucked out,
and Goodstone Aircraft Company made him Lead Man.
Now it's his JOB
to give advice and guidance to me,
so of course he never does.

The Solution

When a Goodstone Aircraft Company machine operator
starts spending most of his 8 hours
asleep in front of his machine
or badmouthing
the quality of the supervision and the aircraft,
Goodstone Aircraft Company makes that man a foreman.

Suddenly the man experiences Enlightenment:
it is obvious that it is actually the machine operators
who aren't worth a shit.

He should know.

It Figures

The supervisors
who are the most cynical about Goodstone Aircraft Company
are the ones who enforce its rules
the most vigorously.

Motivation

I was sitting on a wood bench,
feeding asbestos into a punch press
and punching out asbestos gaskets.
I heard the familiar sound of the foreman's shoes
scraping across the concrete floor of the factory.
I looked up.
The foreman was standing next to my machine,
staring down at me with his arms crossed in front of his chest.
The foreman tightened the muscles in his arms.
My asshole puckered up.
The foreman smirked
at how helpless and trapped I looked.
The foreman had told me about the men he had seen raped
in the County Jail showers.
He had told me that I would get raped
if I went to County Jail,
because I was 22 and obviously a virgin.
I was terrified that I would lose my job
and get into trouble and go to jail,
and the foreman knew this.
The foreman put his tongue in his cheek and leered at me.
It was the same leer he had given me
the time he had threatened to fire me if I didn't work faster.
The foreman kept leering at me
and I could feel the cold shower walls of County Jail
and I began to feed the asbestos faster,
my fingers jumping back
from the steel cutting edge of the die
beneath the asbestos
as my foot hit the pedal that brought the punch press down.
Sweat formed on my skin
and I watched my fingers
to keep from chopping them off
as I fed the asbestos faster, and faster, and faster.
I heard the foreman laugh
and I glanced up and saw him nodding proudly
like he had just reamed me in the ass
for 20 minutes.

Nothing To Lose

I caught the sharp corners
of the foot-square tool steel blocks
with my fingers
as I flipped the blocks in circles
of 90° turns,
then dropped them,
always making my fingers jump out
from under the sharp corners
a millisecond before the blocks slammed
their 40 lb. tool steel weight
onto my milling machine table,
and I
made the white-shirted man's
sweat
pour down his sides and his face
and his neck,
made his eyes pop,
made him pace and circle
my machine
in the steel mill heat and roaring noise
telling me again and again
how I scared him how I made him nervous
how those blocks weren't meant to be tossed around like that I
was
going to smash my fingers,
and I grinned more each day
and my eyes glazed over
and I stared out those high steel mill windows
and flipped the blocks around,
knowing
that I finally had something,
the way I could make that man
hop trotting out of his office to pace
about my machine
in misery
each day.

Power

The foreman has wanted to fire me for a long time.

The foreman stares at me
with contempt and malice
as he paces around my machine,
running his eyes up and down
every inch of my body.
His fists clench
like he wants to pound the steel machine table
in front of my face.

My first word of defiance to him,
the first punch I hit him with,
and he will have me fired.

But I will never give the foreman that victory,
because as I work
I think about the mountains outside the machine shop,
and they give me the strength I need
to resist the foreman's provocations.
The mountains are more powerful than he is.

They will outlast him.

A Warm Body

I am taken off my regular machine
and sent to another building
where the supervisor
puts me on machine #613.
The supervisor looks panicky
and rushes away
before I have a chance to prove
that he knows nothing about the machine
or how the work is done on it,
and I am left
staring at a machine I have no idea how to operate,
staring at an inscrutable blueprint to some job
left half undone,
knowing that the only other man at Goodstone Aircraft Company
who could help me with the job
didn't come to work today.

But I am not worried.
The supervisor and I both know
that as a Goodstone-trained employee
I am an expert
at figuring out how to look
like I'm accomplishing something
when I'm not.

Authority

If a Goodstone Aircraft Company supevisor
puts you on a machine you hate to operate,
don't let him know that you hate to operate it,
or he may never take you off it.
Whatever you do,
don't let him know which machine
you really like to operate.
He'll never put you on it again.

Goodstone Aircraft Company has become aware of the
fact that I am
that rarest of rare birds in the machine shop:
I am actually competent, and highly productive,
on my Bridgeport milling machine.
They have taken immediate advantage of the fact,
and more and more often
I find myself being presented with
penciled drawings of
desktop ash trays and sign holders,
car parts, tools,
latches, hinges, handles
for people's cars, refrigerators,
windows—
all of those supervisors and managers
and office personnel
really know how to make the most of
a good employee.

Insomnia

Supervisor Rooks wasn't letting Conrad sleep
at his machine any more.
Rooks was
jumping out from behind cabinets or posts
or sneaking up behind Conrad
to wake him up in the leather swivel chair
beside his machine
with screaming insults and threats
about busting him from a Grade 16
milling machine machinist
down to a Grade 3 de-burrer
who would suck up metal dust all day
grinding chamfers onto bomber parts
with vibrating screaming hand grinders
over in building 51
where the average IQ was 40 points lower.
Conrad was going to have no part of it.
He took to carrying
a long curved sailor's knife in a sheath on his hip
and he kept pulling it out
and flashing it
whenever he was sure Rooks was watching,
darting about his machine in his long open
cape-like overcoat
with his bugged bloodshot eyes
and his beret on.

He still did almost no work,
but at least he wasn't going to make Rooks look so bad
if some Goodstone Aircraft Company bigshot
took a surprise walk
through the shop.

Whipped

The foreman drove a truck with 4' high
BIG BOSS BRUISER tires
on it
and he liked to come at a man in his machine shop
with his fists out and circling up and over each other
in front of his face ready to fight
whenever a man said the wrong thing to him,
he was a BIG man and he
told his wife when to shut up and give him a blowjob,
punching her eye
every once in a while—
until he got his hand caught in the machine
that tore the skin off it and twisted it
and 2 months later
he was curled up next to his wife like a baby
crying all over her
because he didn't think
he'd be able to beat up his men any more.

Little Hitler

I.C. the lathe Lead Man
would stand like a ramrod
and let out an ear-piercing fingers-in-mouth whistle,
yelling "Hey, GUY!"
at one of his men when he wanted him,
his right arm held out from his side
and extended straight down with his finger
pointing at a spot on the concrete floor
beside him,
his jaw stuck out and his eyes furious
as he waited for the man to run over
and stand on the spot he was pointing at.
The Jesus freaks,
martyred
and muttering, "Just like a sheep to the slaughter"
to machinists as they passed
would always rush right over to the spot and stand there
leaning their ears
toward I.C.'s big mouth,
while the bikers laughed at him,
snapping to attention and saluting and screaming out,
"Right away, SIR!"
or whistling the "Marine Hymn" or "Stars and Stripes Forever"
and then ignoring him,
yelling, "Hey, GUY!"
at each other from machine to machine
all day
whenever they wanted each other's attention.

At The Lazy G Ranch

I always wait
at my machine with nothing to do for an hour or two, for as
long as I can possibly stand it
before breaking down and tearing off
in bored desperation searching for my Goodstone Aircraft
Company
Lead Man again,
finding him and startling him
out of lazy leaned-up-against-a-post
conversation with workers
about golf games
and waterskiing
and which roads to take on motorcycle trips
up the coast,
and he keeps jumping as he sees me
suddenly standing there
before him with my eyes pleading
for work,
he keeps shooting angry and wounded glances at me
that make me feel
like some slavedriving boss.

When a machinist sticks his arm up into the air
and waves for help to his Lead Man who is standing
50 feet away in a conversation about his golf game
with the layout man,
and the Lead Man grins and waves back
to the machinist sarcastically as if
he were just saying "hi"
and were never going to help the machinist,
the machinist can relax
knowing the Lead Man will be there in 5 or 10 minutes
to help,
but if the Lead Man responds
by upraising his hand
along the side of his face with middle finger prominent
in such a way
as to suspiciously suggest
the flipping of the bird
to the machinist,
the machinist had better get ready to grab his newspaper
and go find a bathroom stall to sit in
for half an hour.

Consideration

The machinist's supervisor
stands right next to the machinist
as the machinist airs a complaint
about the working conditions,
leaning his ear toward the machinist's mouth
and nodding,
a look of deep concern and intense concentration
furrowing his brow as he says, "Uh huh! Yes, Bob, yes!"
over and over
as the machinist talks,
after a while taking a deep breath
and shifting his weight
and leaning his ear extra close to the machinist and saying,
"SURE, Bob, SURE! Uh huh, un huh, yes Bob, yes!" over and over
with extra-emphatic nodding jerks
of his head.

It's the least he can do,
considering
it all goes in one ear and out the other.

Loss Of Morale

Whenever we asked our Lead Man a question
regarding why Goodstone Aircraft Company did something the
way it did,
he'd go into his head-shaking
eyes lifted toward the ceiling
smirk
and begin jacking off that big
imaginary erection in front of the fly
of his jeans,
as he walked around the shop
telling us stories of managerial kickbacks and negligence
and incompetence,
getting thinner and thinner
as he ate less and less
until he was down to one small carton of yogurt
a day,
sitting motionless on his stool in front of his toolbox all day,
pale and bone-thin with eyelids half open.

Finally Medical arrived
to carry him out on a stretcher
passed-out and white as a sheet.

He couldn't even qualify
as a warm body
anymore.

Why Waste Your Time?

Our Lead Man always said
that he hung his brain outside the machine shop door
before he came in
to Goodstone Aircraft Company each day
to work,
and whenever one of us would question him
about WHY Goodstone did
one of the many insane and incredibly stupid things
it was always doing,
he'd just raise his eyes to the ceiling
50 feet above and look disgusted as he
began stroking that big invisible hard-on
in front of his pants fly
again,
reminding us one more time
what the untimate reasoning and governing principles around
that place
amounted to.

Disadvantage

The supervisor jabbers and screams
about how the machinist should do the job.
The supervisor throws parts around,
jams his fists into his pockets
and pumps himself up and down on the balls of his feet,
his face red
as he huffs and puffs.

But the machinist is calm,
listens politely and attentively to the supervisor,
waits for him to finish.

The machinist knows that the supervisor has a rough job,
having to somehow compensate
for the fact that he is supervising men
who for 20 years or more have run machines
that he has never run once
in his life.

Siberia

Occasionally
our Goodstone Aircraft Company supervisors will
send us over to the machine shop 700 yards away
in the far corner of building 99
to work for a night or two,
leaving us to wonder what it is that we have done
wrong.
The machinists in building 99
are edgy,
uncontrollably grinning
or giving thumbs-up signs
or whistling circus melodies—
the fuses in their brains
blown
as they wander and reel away from their machines
to sneak up behind each other
and rattle metal or bang hammers,
scaring the shit out of each other,
hovering incessantly
in each other's way,
looking over each other's shoulder
and chuckling
at each other's
intense, nerve-wrenching job concentration—
doing everything in their power
to drive each other to the brink
of snapping,
while the supervisor fumes and struts about
in a red white and blue jacket
covered with military epaulets,
screaming about getting the competition
by the balls.

Manly

In the tiny trailer
on the back of the lot behind the gasket factory
the Vice President sat on a stool
in front of his drafting board at the window
as I bent steel rule at the other end of the trailer.
He told me
his story of how the Vikings
from whom he was descended
used to love to cut a man's chest open
and pull his lungs out as fast as possible
so that they would still be breathing, moving
in the air outside the man as the man died.
"They called them angel wings," he said. "They liked to see
them flap,"
and he stuck his chest and jaw out
proudly
and pulled out his wooden model
of a Wild West pistol
and sanded it
lovingly,
until the bitterness entered his eyes as the men from the factory
came into the trailer again
with another steel rule die for me to fix
and made their usual jokes
about the Vice President's fat wife
and how he couldn't get it up any more.

Wild Goose Chaser

The man from the offices
in the white shirt with the clipboard
looks apologetic and embarrassed
like someone doing something insane
as he pokes his head around in the air
looking at the 6E building column code
on the steel-beam post rising out of the concrete
in back of our Bridgeport machines,
and keeps his eyes on his clipboard as he says
that he was told to check whether or not
Bridgeport machine #491263001
located at column 6E of building 29
had been removed from building 29
yesterday,
nodding his head obsequiously as if to say, "Of course,"
as we tell him that not only have our Bridgeport machines
been there for years,
but that neither of them
has serial number 491263001.

The managers are paid
to call the machinists up into the conference rooms
and tell them
how desperately
a crib for tooling in the machine shop
is needed,
how much new nuts and bolts
and chucks and vises
are needed,
and how very much they want the machinists to have these
things,
how in fact it has been decided
that the machinists WILL have these things.
The fact that the managers
and all of the veteran machinists
know
that the machinists never will have those things
doesn't seem to discourage the managers
at all.

The managers know they're doing their job.

The Standard of Excellence

The Air Force provides Goodstone Aircraft Company
with an S.A.P. AUDIT book.
The book tells the Goodstone Aircraft Company machinists
exactly which questions the Air Force's S.A.P. AUDIT
will ask and what the machinists' answers should be.
The book delineates all of the specifications and
regulations that the machinists have never abided by.
It tells the machinists exactly
how the shop should have been run
for the past 3 years,
so that the machinists can execute a crash
15-day cram session
on manufacturing orders and blueprints,
machine speed and feed calculations,
cleanliness and safety standards,
and tooling and material identification.

Our machinists will be proficient and efficient
and clean and safe.

Pride

The supervisor tells us that the Air Force
will have auditors in the building walking around
watching us,
so that if we are going to walk around the shop
doing nothing
like we usually do,
we should at least carry manufacturing orders
in our hands,
and if we are going to gather at each other's machines
to bullshit,
we should bullshit with blueprints in our hands.
Also,
we should open those Goodstone Manufacturing Standards
books and find out what those funny looking symbols
and numbers on the blueprints
mean to tell us
about dimensional tolerances and standards,
just in case the auditors ask us questions about them.

I guess if we're going to be the morons and liars and
thieves that the supervisor has always said we are,
at least we can be Air Force approved
morons and liars and thieves.

"The Cowboy" was the manager of the machine shop
at Goodstone Aircraft Company.
He wore cowboy boots and a 10-gallon hat
as he walked tall like Ronald Reagan
around the machine shop,
eating jelly beans
he grabbed out of a bowl on a counter
above the supervisor's desk.

The machinists dressed somewhere between "Top Gun"s
and "Rambo"s,
wearing military brown and green camouflage
pants and hats,
black high-top military boots
flight jackets
and aviator sunglasses.

Too bad that the K-20 nuclear bombers
they were making
were for real.

Idealist

The manager is very dedicated and concerned
about walking the aisles
looking for parallel bars and angle plates
and adjustable knees
and chucks
that are stored out on workbenches or
cabinet tops
within easy reach of machinists
who use them continuously and like to know
exactly where they are,
conscientiously yelling
to supervisors about making the machinists
put the tooling away in the cabinets and racks
way down the aisle
in the cage at the end of the building,
so that
it will be terribly difficult and inconvenient and time consuming
for the machinists to find or get
the tooling,
tireless in his pursuit
of another award from the Air Force
for what they call
good housekeeping.

Gung Ho

The biker,
our new parts inspector,
finds the most exciting and prestigious
part of his job
to be the fearless ways he finds to spend 80% of his time—
the way
he kicks back in his leather swivel chair
with hungover eyes and 3 days' growth of beard,
propping his long legs up on the granite
inspection table with his hands behind his head
and letting out
with yawns that he lets rip at the loudest possible volume,
protracting them as long as possible
and then ending them as screaming hoots
that echo off the ceiling 50 feet above,
the way
he blasts heavy metal music
through wires into his ears
and dances about the granite table
or takes out his 4" square
portable television
and sets it right in the middle of the table
and watches it—
becoming really inspired
and getting his biggest thrills
going out of his way
to add special touches
of super-blatancy
and extra-defiant facial expressions
whenever the branch manager or an Air Force official
walk by.

Flair

The first article parts inspector
likes to call his indicator holder
made up of a particularly complex and awkward
set of rods and couplings and clamps
"a whore's nightmare,"
while a first article part that checks out precisely
within the tolerance and shines with smooth finish
he calls "pussy good."
A dimension that is held
to the exact thousandth of an inch
he likes to call "dead nuts,"
while a dimensional tolerance that
is undercut by a few thousandths
has missed by "a cunt hair."

The inspector especially likes that
38" 23" 36" drill press operator
to bring her first article part over
so he can "check her hole."

How To Be Happy

My Lead Man
had perfected the art of not thinking.
He raced about our machines whistling
his imitation of our machine cutters
slicing through metal
as he stamped aircraft parts conformance cards
without checking aircraft parts,
frowning if anyone brought up doubts
about aircraft parts being good
and yelling, "Tough shit!" or "Fuck it!"
followed by "We'll send it through and see if it flies!"—
chuckling his patented
sinister chuckle
as his eyes twinkled,
staring hard into the eyes
of particularly hard-case machine operators
who couldn't stop worrying
and telling them to "Pray a lot!"—
throwing their parts
into the box to be taken away
and telling them cheerfully,
"The only thing you want to worry about is whether or not
you get paid on Friday!"

Quandary

I knew it was going to take me a long time
to decide whether or not to worry
about the 2 Lead Men
who laughed when I asked them if a breakout
point I'd cut 1/4 inch off target was okay,
the first saying, "Sure—just hope it ain't something that
holds the wing on—but hey! if it falls off, it falls off!"—
the second nodding in agreement and adding,
"Sure hope it don't fly over my house!"

Proven

I am left wondering and
tilting my head back and forth and scratching my chin
as I stare in disbelief at a blueprint's
tangent and target points and breakouts and lines
that don't make sense
and its dimensions
that don't add up,
until I finally exhaust my ability
to waste time going over and over the blueprint
that I know I will never understand
and have my Lead Man
call an engineer,
who arrives several hours later
to stare at the print and tilt his head
back and forth and scratch his chin
and say that, yeah,
I could take those lines or dimensions
either way,
that hey,
yeah that sure is an ambiguous fucked-up blueprint,
then signing the print and stamping
"Use As Is" on it
like countless engineers
before him have.

The fact that
the blueprint's been used for 15 years of aircraft manufacturing
is obviously proof enough
that it's okay.

Bobby
still spends a lot of time and energy
making sure those slots he cuts through the ends of
the tubes
are no more than 5 thousandths of an inch away
from perfect
depth and width,
but he does wonder a bit
ever since
he took that tube with the slots
he'd accidentally cut 30 thousandths too wide
down to the inspector
and the inspector had inspected it
and shrugged and said, "NO PROBLEM!"
as he stamped the first article conformance chart box
with his stamp
signifying a good part.

Do Or Die

I was cutting slots into hinges,
trying to hold the plus or minus two thousandths of an inch
tolerances on the slots,
but the other shift had already cut the overall length of the hinges
down to size,
and there was no extra tolerance to play with,
so I was unable to come close to holding
the plus or minus two thousandths on the last slots.
Thinking the hinges were now all
"non-conforming material" destined for the scrap bin,
I called my foreman over
and told him the sad truth.
But he looked at the parts and the print
and smirked and slapped the print with the nails of 2 fingers
and said, "Ah, they'll buy 'em, they'll fly 'em out of here—
those tolerances are MICKEY MOUSE!"

Something was wrong,
but having worked at Goodstone Aircraft Company for 7 years,
I knew enough not to wonder
what it was.

He is worried,
so he tells his foreman about
the 65 titanium forgings
made out of 65 different lots of titanium.

65 forgings,
each with the titanium lot number machined off it.
65 titanium lot numbers on tags
mixed up and tied with wire to the wrong forgings.
65 forgings that he will machine into 65 fuselage shoulder braces
that will be incorrectly matched
with the results of the ultrasonic stress tests
upon the lots of titanium.
65 fuselage shoulder braces
that could fracture under stress
in flight.

"Don't worry about it," the foreman says,
putting a hand on his shoulder. "It happens all the time."

The Routine

Jorge had been running the same job for years,
milling the sides and the inside trough
of aluminum I-beam-shaped K-20 bomber spars,
arranging plastic tubing in grooves on a vacuum plate
with a rubber hammer,
then throwing the switch opening the valve
to the vacuum plate
causing the spars to be sucked down tight so that
he could run them through the 4-inch-wide mill cutter
and the 1-inch-thick stagger-toothed side cutters
like grass through lawnmower blades,
sending up stinking clouds of
coolant smoke and producing a finished
spar, except
for all those times when he forgot to
arrange the plastic tubing
or throw the switch opening the vacuum plate valve.
Then his spacey eyes
would suddenly turn huge and bugged
as his mouth dropped open
and the razor-sharp spar was launched like a spear
flying at 100 m.p.h. off his machine table
and up through the air and into the corrugated tin partition
Lefty
always had strategically placed between his machine
and Jorge's.
Then Jorge would always express the greatest wonder
and disbelief
at how in the world that could have happened to him
again,
and Lefty would come up out of his crouch shaking and
peeking around the partition
to tell Jorge for the umpteenth time
that he should have been a janitor.

To position the 1/2-ton wing carry-through sections
on our machine tables,
our Lead Man
was always grabbing the 50 lb. lead hammer
we refused to pick up
and holding it like a baseball bat swinging it
extra far back
digging his toes in throwing his entire body into it
and driving the head of the lead hammer
SMACK into the side of the titanium carry-through section
that would join wings
and fuselage of a K-20 bomber,
as we remembered what we had been told
about never touching the sections
with lead hammers at all
because the lead contaminated the titanium
and caused cracks and imperfections
up to an inch beneath the surface
of the titanium.

Of course,
that was before
they'd found a big pile of fucked-up wing carry-through
sections hidden in back of building 75
that had to be finished and delivered to the Air Force
right away.

Sometimes you can't afford
to be too picky.

Making The World's Most Advanced Bomber

The operators tried to make the machines
guide the half-ton bomber parts
into the razor-sharp cutters.

The old, worn-out machines rocked
as if they were about to tip over
under the weight of the bomber parts.
Gears ground and engines smoked
as the machines knocked and rattled inside,
starting and stopping without warning.

The foreman paced the aisles with terror in his eyes.

The operators avoided the machines.
They read newspapers in the bathroom,
shuffled back and forth from the vending machines,
and ran their fingers through piles
of old, stripped T-bolts

as they wondered what Goodstone Aircraft Company was doing
with the money
from its billion-dollar Air Force contract.

The Air Force wanted the machine shop "legal"
so the Goodstone Aircraft Company foremen combed
the building,
clearing out cabinets and drawers
of all tooling fixtures
that were "illegal"
because they had been made before the Air Force
contract,
leaving the drawers and cabinets very legal
and very empty
as they threw all of the "illegal" tooling out.
This left the machinists
with piles of very legal
blocks
and clamps
and nuts and bolts
with which they could waste a great deal of time
trying to replace the fixtures
with mickey mouse,
inadequate
set-ups.

Things were definitely going to be done
the Air Force way.

The Purge

The Christians
at Goodstone Aircraft Company spend their lunch breaks up
in the conference room
having discussions about the Anti-Christ
and demons,
then come down the stairs
into the machine shop with beady eyes
and smug smiles to look for
demons
and workers possessed by them,
ready to exorcise them
out of this otherwise
fine workplace
full of hundreds of machines and men
toiling to produce
K-20 nuclear bombers.

At Goodstone Aircraft Company

The blacks and the bikers
operated machines next to each other.

The bikers yelled nigger jokes to each other
and plastered their rollaway toolboxes
with Confederate flag stickers.

The blacks had anxiety attacks
and read Bibles
and found the hangman's nooses that the bikers hung
from the beams above the blacks' machines.

But the blacks and the bikers rose above this and united
in their dedication to making the K-20 bombers
that would carry atomic bombs
and thus ensure peace for all.

We are supposed to cut weld preparations
along cracks in diffusion-bonded wing carry-thru sections
found piled outside Department 88,
so that welders can fill the cracks with titanium weld.

The Air Force wants the wing carry-thru sections NOW,
but we keep asking questions
about the unclear weld preparation blueprints.

Our foremen try to end our questions
by reading the blueprints upside-down
and giving us obviously bad advice.
They are beginning to avoid us
by hiding in the offices or walking laps
around the inside of the building.
When we press them, they refer us to supervisors
who shake their heads and refer us to manufacturing
engineers who shake their heads and carry the blueprints
into engineering offices which send the blueprints back
to us unchanged or even more unclear.

"JUST CUT IT!" the foremen scream at us.

We are beginning to feel uneasy.
We are beginning to wonder about those jokes
about the wings falling off the bombers.

For the first time in our careers, Goodstone Aircraft
Company has made us feel like responsible adults.
There must be something seriously wrong.

On the horizontal mill in the back corner
we machined slots into the hinges
of escape hatches,
slots that would allow the escape hatches
to swing open
when Air Force crew members had to bail out
of crashing K-20 bombers.
With excruciating craftsmanship and care,
we used shimstock and C-clamps
and rubber mallets
to position the hatches,
taking days
to shave thousanths of inches
off the sides of slots
with saw cutters,
closing micrometers and running indicators
all over the surfaces of the slots
to make sure that they were as near to perfect
as possible.

We all knew
that if there were one K-20 bomber part
that would truly be indispensible to the preservation of
American lives,
it would be the escape hatch.

Making America Strong

We worked nights as machine operators
at Goodstone Aircraft Company, where we made parts
for the Air Force's new bomber, the K-20.
In the parking lot, before work and during lunch break,
we drank and smoked dope and snorted chemicals.
At work we wore sunglasses
and danced in front of our machines.
We picked up bomber parts and blew through them
as if they were saxophones.
We stalked each other with squirt guns,
screaming and laughing and staggering.
We played with the overhead crane,
hoisting each other's tool boxes to the ceiling.
We unscrewed knobs from machine handles
and threw them around like baseballs.
Our foreman snuck drinks
from the bottle of Vodka in his toolbox,
and paced about the shop in a daze.
We respected our foreman.
He'd given us some valuable advice.
"Whatever you do," he'd warned us over and over, "don't join
the Air Force and fly a K-20. It's gonna CRASH."

In the Goodstone Aircraft Company machine shop bathroom
at the end of each shift
we would butt elbows jockeying
to get to the sinks.
"Let a WORKING man through!"
inevitably brought raucous laughter, as did
"Boy, I really WORKED today!"
We would all smile and laugh and shake our heads
as we washed.
"How'd you get dirty, you fall off your stool?"
"People have been put in jail for stealing less money than
I do working here!"
"Yeah, I feel guilty when I stand in line to cash
my paycheck!"
Slapping and bumping each other in front of the mirror
with our $16 an hour grins.
"Well, we fooled 'em again!"

Goodstone Aircraft Company imposes
a mandatory overtime schedule,
and the machinists soon
slow down
until they are putting out less
production than they were putting out
before the overtime started.

But Goodstone Aircraft Company keeps on with the overtime
for months,
falling further and further behind in production
as it pays the machinists big overtime bucks.

It's not easy,
spending all of that money
the Air Force keeps giving Goodstone Aircraft Company
each year.

Conscientious

The mentally healthy
machinist
has bloodshot, stoned-hungover eyes.
He staggers slightly and smiles
a devil-may-care smile
as he throws tools around and chuckles,
saying, "Good enough for the government"
over and over
as he barely checks the parts he has machined,
then tosses them onto the finished parts pile.
The mentally ill
machinist
walks about with his hair perfectly combed,
wearing a neat ironed work uniform,
sober as a judge,
laying his tools out like surgical equipment
on a white towel he has spread across
his workbench,
and wearing a plastic wrap-around
magnifying glass headset
in front of his eyes
as he peers at parts and calipers and blueprints
for hours,
all the time keeping that latest RL-600
plane crash
that killed 303 people
in the back of his mind.

Rallying

Every 6 months or so
Goodstone Aircraft Company spreads rumors
throughout the machine shop that it is selling out
to the Japanese,
and the insides of the bathroom stall doors
fill up again
with drawings of big slant-eyed heads talking about
taking over the U.S.
and indignant statements blaming it all
on people who buy Toyotas and Datsuns,
along with various fervent wishes ranging
from "kill all nips" to
"time to warm up the Enola Gay again."

It's as close to a defense of Goodstone Aircraft Company
as the machinists ever get.

Playing Rough

Now that the new union contract talks are approaching,
Goodstone Aircraft Company
has begun really cracking down.
They're putting dents into the lucrative workplace drug
dealing by actually busting people,
they're questioning why certain people
seem to be riding around all day on those electric
stand-up scooters with nothing to do
but give girls rides,
they're actually frowning on machine operators
leaning back in leather swivel chairs with their feet
up on workbenches
doing nothing,
they're even letting the overhead tube lights
in the bathroom stalls
go dim or out
so that we won't be able to sit there for hours
reading newspapers.

I guess they're just trying to make us appreciate them,
by reminding us
what a real job is like.

Of Course

There is a very logical and good reason
why we machinists
drag our sawed-in-half 100 gallon oil drum chip barrels
by their ropes
all the way down the main aisle and out the back door
down the back of the building to empty them
into the big chip dumpsters
at the end of each shift
even if there is only a thimble-full
of metal chips
in them—
it's the way those next-shift supervisors
come in frantically
spending their first half hour
craning their necks and poking their heads about
as they dart around posts and machines
sticking their noses down toward chip barrels
looking for the tiniest piles of chips,
whirling about
poking the air with their fingers and screaming
indignation and anger
if they find them,
because their jobs depend on it.

Philosophical

The night shift Lead Man
comes in to find a pile
of 12 parts
cut undersized and therefore
useless junk destined
for the scrap metal dumpster.
He runs his thumb across them
and gazes lovingly
at the 12 bars of new material
stacked on the workbench,
knowing that they mean
2 more weeks of work,
smiling and nodding his head
and saying, "Job Security."

Goodstone Aircraft Company
has just been awarded several huge multi-billion dollar contracts
that should guarantee work
for years and years to come,
so naturally it immediately calls the machinists
into the office
to show them a company videotape
of the company president telling them that
they are lucky he didn't go ahead and sell the company
like he was thinking of doing,
and that they had better do their job right
on these new contracts
or they will find themselves without a job
real soon.

"There will be no layoffs!"
the supervisor yelled at us
during the monthly shop talk.
A month later we were asking him,
"What about the secretaries they just laid off?"
and he was yelling at us,
"There will be no layoffs on the shop floor!"
Another month later we were asking him,
"What about the inspector and the toolmaker they just
laid off?" and he was yelling at us,
"There will be no layoffs in DIRECT production!
You guys are DIRECT production! Wait'll you see what
happens when we get that Weber Co. construction contract
next month; boy, we'll have TWICE as much work; you
guys think it's busy now, wait'll . . . "
Another month later the supervisor was passing out slips
of paper to us.
"Why do they want me in the office at 11:00 a.m.?" I was
asking him.
"I don't know. Maybe you got a phone call."

In the office they were smiling at us.
"We very well MIGHT call you back in a month. We can't
promise anything, but keep us informed of any address
changes, because we very well MIGHT . . . "

FRED VOSS dropped out of the UCLA Ph.D. program in English Literature In 1974 to turn his eyes and soul out toward life and its real people, working as a Hollywood busboy, a steel-rule die maker, a steelcutter in a steel mill, and a machinist in various machine shops, while writing novels and then poetry.

Fred's first chapbook, *Goodstone Aircraft Company,* was rated "a classic" by Marvin Malone, editor of *Wormwood Review,* and has been called " . . . flat-out one of the best two or three collections of on-the-job poems I've ever seen, 29 pages of cover-to-cover, can't-put-it-down reading . . . "by Merritt Clifton, editor of *Samisdat* magazine.

John Osborne, professor in the American Studies Department of the University of Hull in England and editor of the British literary magazine *Bête Noire,* has written that Voss' poems about work constitute a "long poem whose directness of address to factory experience is without parallel in contemporary Anglo-American verse."